Bound 3/31/76

PFLAUM / STANDARD
38 West Fifth Street, Dayton, Ohio 45402

**POP CULTURE**

arthur asa berger

Library of Congress Catalog Card Number 72-94558
© 1973 Arthur Asa Berger

For Permissions and Sources see page 192.
ISBN 0-8278-0023-1
10023/3.1M/S6M-2-973

Acknowledgements

I deeply appreciate the unselfish
labor of Barbara Clifford, Patty
Gary, and Lorraine de la Fuente,
who did most of the manuscript
typing. I have also been encouraged
by the interest and work of many
of my pop culture students and am
grateful to the members of my department and to the faculty and
administration of California State
University, San Francisco, for
various small favors and the good-
natured way in which they toler-
ated me and my seemingly eccentric
concerns.

Book Design : Joe Loverti
Photography : Paul Tucker
Illustrations : Arthur Asa Berger

# CONTENTS

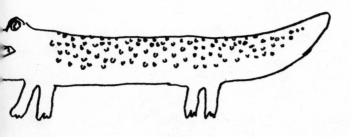

Common Objects and Everyday Activities

Styles, Symbols and Social Phenomena

Cameos

# WHAT IS POPULAR CULTURE, AND
# WHY IS IT IMPORTANT FOR US TO UNDERSTAND IT?

One of the curious things about popular culture is that, though almost everybody spends his life immersed in it, nobody seems able to agree about what it is. We glance at the comics daily. That's popular culture. We watch television a good deal. (Statistics reveal the average family television set is on about five hours a day.) That's a *heavy* dose of popular culture. We go to the movies, buy rock and roll records, eat snacks, and dress in certain ways. All of this is popular culture, as I think of it.

Some people make a distinction between *popular arts*, such as detective stories, westerns, and situation comedies, and *mass media*, such as radio, television, film, newspapers and magazines. But since so much of the media is full of the popular arts, the distinction between the two doesn't seem to be that important.

Some people talk about mass culture, which suggests they are interested in the "culture" of the ordinary man (as contrasted with the "high culture" of the elite). But the title of an important collection of articles on mass culture, published in the mid-fifties, was *Mass Culture: The Popular Arts in America*, which suggests that mass culture and the popular arts are the same thing.

In the absence of agreement on what popular culture, the popular arts, or mass culture may be, I will offer my own definition. (I prefer the term popular culture not only because it is the most widely accepted description of what we are talking about, but also because it seems to me the most accurate.)

Popular culture, to me, is broader than the popular arts. It is the culture of the people—their behavior, values, and, in particular, their entertainments, and not just certain art forms which appeal to large numbers of people. Perhaps the best thing to do is to indicate what popular culture generally is not. It is not the classic works of literature and philosophy, though curiously enough much popular culture is related directly to the same myths as Greek tragedy, for instance. It is not highly sophisticated art which appeals *only* to a person of highly cultivated and discriminating tastes. This kind of person may enjoy modern poetry as well as roller derby and professional football, but the average roller derby and football fan probably doesn't enjoy esoteric poetry or the novels of Henry James.

Regardless of whether or not you like popular culture, the fact that millions of people do, and spend a great amount of time and money on it, means that it is significant. It offers us a useful way of under-) (standing one's society, and, indirectly, oneself. In addition, studying popular culture (that is, looking at it critically in an attempt to interpret it, evaluate it, and understand its impact on society) is fun. Whatever else you may wish to say about popular culture, it has an intoxicating dynamism to it; it is vital, and it is immediate. We've all been affected by it, whether we recognize this or not.

We learn from all of our experiences, and since popular culture is so large a part of our experience, it is only logical to recognize that it must have a considerable impact upon us. Popular culture shapes all of us to varying degrees. We sing songs about love or war, we watch programs or read books in which various kinds of heroes, reflecting a number of different cultural values, act in certain ways—and from all of this we learn. We pick up notions almost by osmosis, so it seems, about how to act with members of the opposite sex, about what "life" is about, about what to wear and eat and do.

( And much of what we do and think and eat and wear is affected by ) popular culture. Therefore, studying popular culture is fascinating and gratifying, because in analyzing popular culture we can learn a great deal about ourselves. Perhaps some of the roles, fantasies, notions, ideas, and values we get from popular culture are harmful and destructive of our happiness and well being. For instance, do television advertisers exploit our fears? Do some songs simplify experience and create unrealistic fantasies? Do certain television programs overstimulate us and expose us to excessive violence?

This book attempts to answer questions of this nature. It looks at a number of aspects of popular culture in an analytical manner, pointing out how they affect our psychological development, our behavior, and the social order.

At times this book is fanciful and even frivolous, but even then I trust it is revealing about our lives and helpful to an understanding of ourselves and our society. And if I can do that best by writing about comics, advertising, wrestling, football, jokes, snacks, and that kind of thing, why shouldn't I?

## THE POOP ON POP

A student in one of my pop culture courses once came up to me and said, "How do you do it? I look at something and it doesn't seem to mean anything much, and you take the same thing and seem to find all kinds of things to talk about." It was just the beginning of the semester, and he hadn't had any exposure to the critical techniques that can be used to analyze and understand pop culture. "Don't worry," I said, trying to reassure him, "in a while you'll be doing the same kind of thing. What you have to do is learn how to play the game." Another student came up to me at the end of one of my courses and said, jokingly, "You've *ruined* my life!" "How?" I asked. "Well," said the student, "I used to be oblivious to all kinds of things—advertisements, and comic strips, television programs and the like—and now, after this blasted course, I seem to analyze everything." These two students represent extremes, and it is quite likely that most students are not as innocent as the first one claimed to be, or as compulsively analytical as the second student claimed to be. The point is, however, that it is possible to develop ways of looking at pop culture in terms of its psychological and social impact. There are two basic methods of investigating pop culture: *you can see what others have written about it* or *you can analyze it yourself*. Sometimes, in making your own interpretation you still will have to call upon the work of others—psychoanalysts, sociologists, and anthropologists, for instance—who have interesting and useful ideas which you can apply to your particular subject. In this book, for instance, you will find numerous occasions where I use insights from people in various disciplines and apply them to pop culture. At times, also, I apply a number of techniques of analysis at the same time. For example, in my essay on Charles Schulz, I dealt with him as a kind of hero who reflects certain fundamental American values. To interpret a comic strip such as *The Fantastic Four* you have to talk about heroes, violence, technology, crime, and a great many other topics. (It took me an entire book to deal with *Li'l Abner* and even then I didn't do as complete a job as I might have.) Following are the more important techniques that can be used for analyzing pop culture and some of the questions asked by people using each technique:

## Historical Development

*When did whatever it is you are investigating get started? How popular or important is it now? Is it different now from the way it used to be? If so, why? If not, how has it resisted change? When was it popular? Was it popular at a particular time for any particular reason?*

Historians are concerned, in essence, with change over a period of time. If pop culture reflects American society, and our society is continually changing, then our pop culture must also be changing. Our new attitudes towards politics and sex, for instance, are reflected in the cinema and in comics; and social historians who don't know about *Young Lust or Zap* can't claim to have a finger upon the national pulse. Long before we started worrying about drug addiction in America we were listening to songs about Mary Jane and White Rabbits, which had special meaning to people in the drug culture or "in the know."

The incredible popularity of football has a "historical" dimension to it, as do the rise of the motel and recent developments in the way we decorate bathrooms. Some of the essays in this book deal with changes that have taken place in American culture while others call attention to interesting events and social movements on the American scene at the present time.

Studying pop culture provides a look at American society from the bottom up, so to speak—in terms of the artifacts (common everyday objects) and entertainments of the ordinary man. Overlooking this perspective, which happens all too often, leads to a distorted view of American culture.

## Comparative Analysis

*Is the same thing done the same way elsewhere? Do different cultures or countries have variations that are interesting? Can we get any statistical information that might be interesting?*

Comparisons are odious, but it is only by making comparisons that we know how to evaluate anything. A family with an income of five thousand dollars a year could live very well in Portugal but in New York this income would barely be above the poverty level. Everything is relative, then. If you think about it, we generally spend a great deal of time comparing things: one football team with another or one movie with another. It's only natural. Sometimes comparisons are interesting. In investigating comics from Italy and America, I found in them rather striking differences in attitudes towards authority, which reflect rather basic differences in attitudes towards authority in the two countries' cultures in general. Different ways of doing the same thing reveal different values and attitudes. There is a world of difference between the TV dinner and French or Italian cooking. Is this because Americans who eat TV dinners have things to do that they consider more important than preparing a well cooked meal? How are cultural differences reflected in differing cuisines? The foods people eat, the language they use, the way they dress and express themselves, the entertainments they prefer —these and many other aspects of life are excellent topics for comparative analysis. And I have used this technique to write about baseball and football, American and Italian comics, differences between hotels and motels as well as other subjects.

### Psychoanalytic Investigation

*Does whatever it is you are studying take care of certain needs we all have? Does it help us deal with anxiety or frustration or anger? Does it reassure us? Calm us? Excite us? What are its functions as far as our "unconscious" is concerned? Is there a difference between its meaning to our unconscious and to what we are conscious of?*

I have been particularly attracted to psychoanalytical analysis because it seems to offer such remarkable insights into the significance of pop culture. I believe that we are generally unaware of the *real* reason we do any number of things—from washing our cars to marrying a particular person. Using the psychoanalytical approach enables me to explain everything from the "real" reason people wash their cars or watch football to the dynamics in *Spider-Man,* or the appeals found in many advertisements.

It is difficult to prove that you are right when you use psychoanalytical notions; I grant this. However, if we are careful to qualify our generalizations and offer evidence to support them—which is something we should do whatever approach we use—I think it is acceptable, and even desirable, to consider pop culture's impact on our individual and collective psyche.

## Sociological Study

*What class levels are appealed to? Does your subject have a racial or ethnic slant to it? Does it appeal to some groups (whether they be of a class, religious, racial, geographic or other group) and not others? Does it have any political significance to it?*

In analyzing pop culture it is wise to remember that there are four basic considerations:

1. The artist; 2. the work of pop culture (art) ; 3. the audience; and 4. America (society).

The sociological approach generally focuses on the relation that exists between the art and the audience, or the artist and America, though it does not neglect other relationships.

For example, during the course of a rather extended conversation with Charles Schulz, the creator of *Peanuts*, about his background, experiences, and ideas, I came to the conclusion that Schulz, as a person, represents and believes in the old "self-made man" ideal in American culture, though his cartoon characters seem to repudiate this ideal.

And when I looked at television wrestling matches I found that these entertainments (they are technically *exhibitions*, not sports) reflect certain views about man and politics, and were, in essence, the "political science" of the lower middle classes, who viewed them. The message of wrestling, aside from the violence, which is disturbing even if comic, is inherently anti-social.

## Myth-Symbol-Ritual Significance

*Can your subject be related in any way to important myths which have either universal or particular (to a country, that is) significance? Does it have a symbolic dimension to it which makes it interesting? Can your subject be looked upon as a kind of ritual?*

This kind of analysis is close to the psychoanalytical approach. The psychoanalysts have done a great deal of work with myths such as those of Adam and Eve and the Garden of Eden which are behind the tendency (extremely strong in America) to see ourselves as "innocents" and "good guys" in a world full of evil and unscrupulous foreigners.

Myths are also behind the notion of the self-made man, and have been incorporated into the identities of many of our culture-heroes, such as the cowboy and the detective.

I should point out that I am using the term myth in its cultural sense —as a legendary story concerning superhuman beings and the creation of the world, and not as an "erroneous belief" or falsehood. I see a relationship between psychological (personal) drives and myths, which I believe often represent "cultural imperatives." The myth is behind the drive which, in turn, is behind various actions we take or things we do, such as washing our cars, buying a pair of Levis, watching football games and football coaches, or buying a package of cereal.

Quite often we are unaware of the myth behind our act, just as we are unaware that our actions often are ritualistic (tightly structured and always done the same way) or have a symbolic significance.

### Content Analysis

*How often (many times per minute, page, episode) is a given kind of behavior (violence, stereotyping of people) observed? What are the basic ideas, values, images and beliefs that are to be found in some publication or program—generally speaking, which is part of a series?*

Content analysis is a way of studying man's behavior by examining comics, magazines, television programs, and other entertainments. The basic concern is to look for *patterns* revealed in several examples of whatever is being investigated. These patterns might have to do with beliefs, attitudes, or behavior—as reflected in language, art forms, and symbols, among other things.

It is important to remember that content analysis is a *quantitative* technique, concerned primarily with the amount of a given thing (such as negative images for Negroes or Jews in popular fiction). Therefore it is important to use this technique only in situations where there is a sizable quantity of material to investigate. You do not do a content analysis of one episode in a comic strip or one issue of a magazine. You can do an excellent content analysis of several months of *Dick Tracy* or a half-dozen issues of *Playboy*. Content analysis reveals themes and general attitudes that are usually not apparent in just one episode of a comic strip or magazine, as my essay on *Authority in the Comics* shows.

The list above does not exhaust the approaches which can be or have been made by people trying to understand and to interpret pop culture. Marxists and Maoists, Jungians and Freudians and neo-Freudians, sociologists, semanticists, literary critics, theologians and many others have probably had something remarkable to say about any subject you might be interested in, and it is wise to do a bit of searching in the library to get some of their ideas. There now exists a number of excellent books on pop culture in general and various kinds of pop culture in particular, and some of our most exciting and interesting writers and scholars have dealt with it, using the various techniques mentioned above.

And fortunately, it is possible to get a pretty good idea of the basic concepts and methods of various disciplines and techniques by reading judiciously. A knowledge of some of the fundamental insights of the psychoanalysts, anthropologists, and historians is enough to get you started with your own analyses of any given topic, though you must always be careful not to oversimplify. If, in addition to your own ideas, you can find an article or two on the same subject (or a related one), you have a sounder basis for judging the validity of your ideas.

A strategy that I often use might be helpful. It is called *Brainstorming*.

## Brainstorming on MISSION IMPOSSIBLE

It is useful sometimes to see what you can come up with just by tossing ideas around in rapid and random fashion. This is called

"brainstorming," and it is used for everything from thinking up new products to planning military operations. Below are examples of the ideas you might develop in brainstorming about the television program *Mission Impossible*.

1. American sense of "mission," which is used in a very literal sense in the program. "Mission," along with "individualism" and "fundamental moral law," are the three keystones of American thought, according to the noted intellectual historian Ralph Henry Gabriel.

2. *Impossible?* Nothing is impossible to Americans, who have incredible technological prowess and courage. Things only *seem* to be impossible.

3. Danger from *foreigners,* who are perennially seeking the mysteries of America or who are engaged in activities which will be harmful to us. We often have to involve ourselves with their activities in their own countries to protect our interests, prevent World War III, etc.

4. We are invulnerable—except for traitors, spies, who can attack from within. This reflects the "conspiracy" theory of history.

5. *Native American genius* versus non-American training . . . in spy academies and military institutes. Devious foreigners can be outsmarted and their brilliance can often be turned against them.

6. *Identity?* This is a fundamental problem of the series for it demonstrates that appearances can deceive. The deus ex machina of the program—the way it often solves problems—is through reliance on disguises and impersonations.

7. *Time and pressure.* The time element is usually the basis for suspense. Will the technological genius (a Negro) and the team be able to do the job in time and without being discovered?

8. *The technological Negro.* Used as a counter to the cliché of the non-cultural, dumb, or menial Negro. Is the technological Negro a counter-cliché? Is he just a fancy janitor?

9. *Sex?* It is very cool. The girl is often a decoy, generally seems quite distant and aloof. This applied to Barbara Bain especially.

Pop Culture/16

10. *All-pervasiveness of the group.* The "team" on *Mission Impossible* is seen as, somehow, "all-powerful." They can infiltrate any defense, place people wherever they need them, get anything done they want done. All they need, generally, is enough time.

11. *Deception the basic category.* There has been little violence on the program. The members of the team tricked people into doing what the "team" wanted them to do by playing identity games, or forced the villains to destroy themselves because of their sexual drives or power drives or both. Later episodes moved away from this trickery tactic and began to adopt the more usual "solution by violence" approach.

12. *The formula. Mission Impossible* seems to have an interesting formula, but are people getting tired of it? How much of the popularity of the program is due to the quality of the acting and the solutions by trickery and technology, and how much to the intellectual quality of the show as a statement about life?

What you see here represents a dozen "educated" thoughts about the program. What else can you come up with? Try to find *specific* things to think about. After you've extended this list on *Mission Impossible,* make up your own list about some other program—or book or comic strip or anything else you might wish to think about.

Once you have brainstormed and have a number of ideas before you, the next step is to devise an intelligent way of organizing this material in some kind of a written statement (theme, essay, review) about it. Also, as I pointed out before, it is always useful to look in the library for articles by experts on your subject which may help you get new ideas or modify some of the notions you got in brainstorming.

Brainstorming and all the techniques discussed can be used in a group or by one person. After you learn how different techniques can be used, you will probably be pleasantly surprised at how much you can "see" in pop culture.

What follows are some of my essays on pop culture and American society which, I hope, you will find both interesting and useful. I see pop culture criticism as a way of fighting against certain negative features of our cultural environment and of gaining a better understanding of ourselves. We watch thousands of hours of television and are exposed to countless advertisements each year. We are bombarded by various kinds of pop culture, and this bombardment must have an effect upon us.

To the extent that we can understand how we are being shaped by our pop culture environment (or, if not shaped, at least affected) we gain a certain measure of freedom and the chance to make decisions for ourselves. It is because autonomy and self-understanding are so important—and so much in danger of being inundated—that I have focused so much attention on what have often been considered rather trivial matters.

I hope you will find this book helpful and entertaining. One of my main arguments is that we learn from our entertainments, so there is every reason to write a book that is entertaining if it can be done.

Pop Culture/19

# AMUSEMENTS AND ENTERTAINMENTS

## THE MAN BEHIND *PEANUTS*—
## 'SPARKY' SCHULZ AND THE AMERICAN DREAM

What kind of person is behind the characters in *Peanuts?* This question must certainly occur to many people as they take their daily glance at the strip. Yet, though he is famous, and could be a great celebrity if he so desired, Charles "Sparky" Schulz has fastidiously kept himself out of the public eye. Even the *Time* cover story about him, which came out in 1965, had his characters and not his own picture on the cover.

I had heard that he lives in the middle of his own golf course and I had even seen him a couple of times on television programs, but his image didn't square very well with his sense of humor. He is what San Franciscans would call "straight": a crew-cut midwesterner who teaches Sunday school and is friendly and decent. An ordinary guy! How do you account for that strange genius for humor? How does a guy like that think up those gags and indulge in such fantastic flights of imagination?

After I met him I found out.

I

Sebastopol, where Schulz lives, is a small city about fifty miles north of San Francisco. It reminded me more of Vermont than California. There are gentle hills and there is a definite "country" but not country-western (which means neon lights and pink motels) quality to the area. It is New England with an eternal spring. I had to stop four or five times to get directions to his place. I'd drive into a gas station and the attendant would say, "Oh yeah, Charlie Schulz, the cartoon man . . ." and give me directions. Finally, after wandering down lonely back roads I found myself before a slight break in the woods—"The Tree Farm." One of those electric gates was barring the way, but as I drove up the driveway it lifted and I entered Schulz's private wonderland. It reminded me, for some reason, of entering the domain of the beast in Cocteau's "Beauty and The Beast." The woods divide (or the gate lifts) and you enter a vast and beautiful garden, except that instead of a formal garden, in the European tradition, you find yourself in the middle of a golf course. A classic study in American practicality. Yet it was only a large informal "garden" of rolling hills punctuated here and there with putting greens. And, it was surprisingly lovely. Nature had been directed but not shaped and civilized as in European formal gardens. The golf course is, we must remember, a kind of nature—generally rough, but not red in tooth and claw, with but few concessions to civilization. What I discovered, after talking with Schulz, is that he is not only a phenomenon (and his impact has been tremendous) but that he is a particularly American phenomenon. He is an *ideal type* and is of interest not only because he is one of our great humorists, though he thinks of himself as a "comic strip artist," but also because of his rather classic Americanism. (In America, people are classical, not gardens.) And what is most fascinating is that it is his Americanism that explains his humor.

As I sat in his studio having coffee and cake with him and talking about comics, American society, his children, and many other things, I couldn't help but admire the beauty of his surroundings. His studio, a California modern rambler on "Charlie Brown Lane," looks out on an idyllic landscape of trimmed fields and clusters of trees. And that, so I have come to believe, is the secret of *Peanuts*—it is an American pastoral.* It is a modernized one, but a pastoral nevertheless. But to explain all this, let us return to Schulz himself.

## II

He is a rather shy person, who sees himself as a man lacking qualities —though he admits to having a sense of humor and being "a genuinely funny person, when you get to know me." This shyness leads him to shun the limelight and, instead, to place his characters there. "When I was in high school," he told me, "I thought I was so ordinary that if I came across a classmate I always assumed I wouldn't be recognized. I thought I was so bland and meaningless." These sentiments are often echoed by Charlie Brown, Schulz's *alter ego*. When you talk with Schulz, however, you find he is a most engaging conversationalist

*Webster's Collegiate Dictionary* defines the pastoral as "a literary work dealing with shepherds or rural life in a usu. artificial manner and typically drawing a contrast between the innocence and serenity of the simple life and the misery and corruption of city and esp. court life."

—with a wide range of interests and an alert mind. Though he is unassuming, he is not as "ordinary" as he makes himself out to be.

The story of his life is one of those remarkable tales that belongs, itself, to the world of comic strips. It is a case study in the American Dream, which started with an advertisement on a book of matches. "My last year in high school I didn't know what to do," he said. "I was never a good student in class and was always uncomfortable in the classroom situation. So there I was—graduating from high school and wanting, more than anything else, to be a cartoonist. My parents wanted to help me but didn't know how. Then, one day, I saw an art school advertised on a matchbook . . . one of those things in which you draw a picture and send it away. It was a correspondence school, the Federal School—now called Art Instruction Schools—in Minneapolis." His high school teacher advised him to go to a regular art school and not to "waste his time" with the correspondence course, but Schulz took it anyhow.

He later became an instructor for the school, correcting lessons and giving the students aid in such things as inking. He is quite proud of his ability with a pen and took out one, an Esterbook radio 914 point, and gave me a demonstration of straight lines, circles and cross-hatches. His first break came when the *St. Paul Pioneer Press* started carrying his cartoons once a week in the Sunday section. He also sold gag cartoons to the *Saturday Evening Post* and eventually got together some strips and, after a persistent effort, managed to get a contract with the United Features Syndicate. "Dedication," he claims, "is the secret of my success."

His first strips were ordinary. Schulz hadn't developed that marvelous line which frees him for his comic extravaganzas, but he was always experimenting. His big break came as a result of a Schroeder cartoon. An editor recognized the music in the cartoon and was amused. He put together a bunch of Schulz cartoons and they sold like crazy. The rest is history. *Happiness Is a Warm Puppy* has sold one million copies. Holt, Rinehart and Winston have sold more than three million copies of his collected cartoons at a dollar each, and Fawcett, which divides the Rinehart books in half and sells them for forty cents, has sold eight million books so far and expects to sell a total of thirty million in the next few years. These figures, which deal with only part of his production, show that Schulz is truly a phenomenon. Because of his cartoons, carried in 800 papers in the United States, books, television shows and the play based on his characters, he is certainly one of the most widely heard voices of the day. More than sixty million people read *Peanuts* every day, and it is popular all over the world.*

He points out, and I think this is a very important consideration, that he does not feel it necessary to please all his readers every day. He loses some readers every day and picks up others. This, plus the fact that the comic strip medium has no end, enables him to experiment a great deal. Most critics of popular culture assume that it must please the "least common denominator," so it cannot be decent—yet *Peanuts* is an example of just the opposite at work. He need not please anyone in particular.

I asked him if he used his cartoons to get a message across. "Yes," he said, "but that is secondary . . . the main thing I try to do in the strip is to amuse people." Since humor does have a social dimension, I asked him if he felt that part of his role was as a critic of American mores and values. He admitted that this was possible and mentioned that a psychiatrist friend had said he was "one of the great social commentators of the times." I asked him about Robert Short's *The Gospel According to Peanuts*. I told him that I believe Short had read a great deal into the cartoons, though it is a well known fact that Schulz is religious, teaches Sunday school (for adults) and has what might be called a "commitment." "I can't really say," he answered. "Short says that he's dealing with *what's there*, and not with what I consciously put into it."

This led to a discussion of religion. Schulz described himself as a "liberal conservative." He is a member of the Church of God, a fundamentalist group, but says that he does not consider himself a funda-

*Recent statistics reveal that more than 1,300 newspapers now carry *Peanuts*. Schulz makes more than three million dollars a year from the strip and its various licensed products.

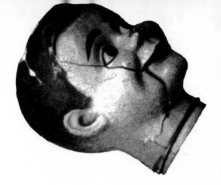

mentalist. He accepts the findings of science. He asked me if I had read Chaim Potok's *Chosen,* which he had just finished. He liked it very much. "If I had to switch my religion, for one reason or another, I'd become Jewish," he told me. He said that he was very sympathetic toward the sufferings of the Jews.

Somehow we got onto the subject of contemporary society. Schulz said that he was upset about the lack of tradition in American life. "The great freedom we have has led to families without any traditions or identity. We've protested everything into nothing." He was rather pessimistic, I felt, about America. He thought that the hippies are repulsive, that they are "offensive to others" in the way they carry on. I had the feeling that Schulz was, in his own way, trying to escape from the complexities of the city. He said that life at Sebastopol was often dull and rather quiet. "There's not much variety here," he said. Yet, if he were in a city he would be bombarded with people, requests for talks and other things, and would find it even harder than he does now to find time for *Peanuts.*

He mentioned that several colleges had wanted to award him honorary doctorates but that he had declined because he doesn't have the time. Though Schulz has secluded himself he is very much tied to the world—with numerous projects occupying his time. He keeps his distance—perhaps because he finds it necessary to do so in order to keep his identity.

III

It is this somewhat ambivalent relation between society and his seclusion in nature that explains *Peanuts'* significance as a pastoral. Since William Empson's influential book, *Some Versions of The Pastoral* (1935), we have come to realize that we can move beyond shepherds frolicking on the grass and still have the pastoral. The pastoral in its modern manifestations can be seen as a device using inversion, and "putting the complex into the simple." At the same time, the old goal of escaping from complexity and the corruption of modern society can be retained.

This is a basic American viewpoint, and to the extent that Americans have identified with and defined themselves in terms of nature and sought to escape complexity, America can be explained in terms of the pastoral. The concept of the self-made man, which lies behind the American Dream, is based on this belief—that man is not a social animal but is some kind of a realization of nature. This definition in terms of nature, which started in America with the Puritans and dominated the nineteenth century, is still with us. It is behind the lemming-like movement to the suburbs and the traditional American fear of "big government." It is, I would guess, behind Schulz's decision to live in Sebastopol, in nature, where, though life is dull, it is not corrupt and corrupting.

There are a number of reasons for describing *Peanuts* as a pastoral comic strip. Perhaps the basic source of humor in the strip comes from Schulz's use of *inversion*: instead of a world of adults we have a world of children and, instead of adopting the convention of the "cute kid," Schulz portrays children as worldly and perhaps even corrupt. The children also act *like* adults—in a society where adults often act like children. And, if you look at the *Peanuts* books, you notice that most of the adventures take place outdoors, in Schulz's rather abstract kind of nature. Schulz told me that for a while he started trying "cute tricks" in the drawings—such as putting in fences and other little details, but he soon gave it up.

Of course he gave it up! Because *Peanuts* relies, to a great degree, upon abstraction and being outside of time and space. There is no society to speak of in *Peanuts*: just modernized shepherds and shepherdesses at play. (Whatever "society" we get—wars, psychiatrists, etc. —is ridiculed.) The basic technique in *Peanuts*, as Schulz himself points out, is to create "isolated incidents in which there is conversation and action by the characters." Occasionally Schulz gets involved with serial adventures, but they tend to tire readers, he said. So even the form, *isolated* incidents, suggests something of the pastoral. And this simplicity and abstractness are reinforced by Schulz's line, that wonderfully economical and fluid line that he uses with such imagination and brilliance. Schulz draws his originals in five and one-half inch boxes, and the line in these originals is somewhat wavy, due to the flexing of the penpoint. But when the originals are reduced to one-and-one-fourth-inch strips, the line is quite beautiful. Schulz likes Linus best of all his characters, though he obviously identifies with Charlie Brown. Charlie Brown's wistful lack of confidence and his tormenting doubts about his identity seem to be derived, though exaggerated, from his creator. But the best character for emergencies, and to my mind the most brilliant of his characters, is Snoopy. "When I'm stuck," Schulz said, "I always turn to Snoopy to get me out of trouble." What is it about Snoopy that is so remarkable? It is, once again, inversion that is behind Snoopy's humor: he is a dog who thinks he is a person. He is, obviously, an unusual dog: a genius, a representative dog, and as brilliant a personality as Ignatz Mouse, the hero of *Krazy Kat,* a strip popular a generation ago. Aside from his humanity, Snoopy is remarkable because of his incredible imagination and his ability to communicate emotions, both verbally and non-verbally.

The first and most evident quality Snoopy has is his humanity—his ability to carry on human relationships. Animals generally treat man as an object, to whom they announce themselves from time to time. Man, for these animals, exists only during these periods and not outside of them. Of course dogs have a certain amount of memory and thus can have relations with humans, but they are relatively primitive. Snoopy, on the other hand, has a completely developed personality—as well as a beautifully equipped doghouse! He participates in history (in fact, he ransacks it) and literature, and has a memory of almost elephantine proportions. He becomes obsessed and monomaniacal, and thus all too human. In Snoopy's compulsions and his heroic efforts, as futile as they are at times, we see ourselves.

The fact that Snoopy is a dog prevents us from taking it all seriously so that nobody takes offense. He is the latest and greatest example of the talking animal convention, which stems from Aesop, and is found in *Alice in Wonderland* and now in numerous comic strips.

The second thing about Snoopy is that he is a dog with "qualities," the most important of which are his fantastic imagination and dogged persistence. There is an existential dimension to Snoopy. Like Sisyphus of old he seems doomed to strive eternally (waging war against the Red Baron) and to have no success. And yet, despite his fate, despite the obvious futility of his situation, he is courageous. He finds his meaning through struggle, not success or failure.

His intoxication with flying and warfare is a reflection of a general preoccupation on the part of Americans with air warfare, missiles, supersonic planes, and the like. He helps us reduce some of our anxiety by turning back the clock, by making us laugh at what, in more modern manifestations, may annihilate us. It isn't as bad as it seems, we tell ourselves. Good fun! We were safe in the era of the Red Baron and would like to be back in those "good old days."

The last thing about Snoopy—and one would have to write a book about him to do him justice—is that he communicates brilliantly. He is a virtuoso of emotions and expresses his feelings not only through language but through gestures, eye movements, posture, facial expressions, his ears, his whole body. He is an extraordinary mimic and not a bad baseball player. The non-verbal aspects of his communication help to confirm impressions we get from his speech and the continuity of the stories so we know precisely what he feels.

Snoopy, then, is a genius—though he wasn't always so. He has changed somewhat over the years. His snout is now longer and his passion greater, yet he must have always had that capacity for development that is behind all self-made men and dogs. Schulz says his greatest ambition is to create a comic strip as good as *Krazy Kat*, perhaps the most outstanding American comic strip produced to date. In *Peanuts*, a felicitous combination of clever gags, incredible characters and beautifully expressive drawing, I think Schulz has come very close to his goal. And the American people, and all the countless others who read him, are all the richer for his efforts. Working in what is essentially an American idiom—the comic strip—Schulz has created something of transcendent and universal value and delight.

## HIPPIES ARE OLD HAT

The existence of the hippies is symptomatic of stresses in the American community, which no longer seems able to provide some segments of the society with moral and psychic support, with a sense of purpose and of obligation. America has had many communities setting themselves apart from what was considered to be a corrupting influence, to form a more perfect social order. Such was the history of Noyes' Oneida community and other nineteenth-century Utopias.

The long hair, elaborate dress, and role playing of the hippies hark back to the Middle Ages when, according to the great historian Huizinga, man faced three ways of coping with existence. He could retreat from life into the monastery, effect social and political reform, or make life a dream. Most men (here we're talking about the upper class, of course) chose the last, since they didn't believe in progress or the possibility of social reform. Such seems to be the case with many of the hippies. But like monks, they see themselves as making up, through the intensity and quality of their love, for the lack of it in the ordinary man. And with their elaborate clothes, they reject the "work suit" which has been man's dress for the past few centuries.

# MARVEL COMICS: LANGUAGE, YOUTH
## AND THE PROBLEM OF IDENTITY

I would like to investigate some of the unique qualities of *The Fantastic Four* and the *Amazing Spider-Man* which we find in Marvel language. What we are doing, really, is looking at the work of Stan Lee, who plots and writes these stories. His innovations in the characterological aspects of the comic book—the flawed hero—and the linguistic aspects—irony, self-parody, and hyperbole—distinguish these two comic books. Some of the other comic books of the Marvel Group, such as *Captain America*, do not have these elements and are as childish and uninteresting as most comic books.

The first thing we notice as we look at a Marvel comic (and I will use this term to mean either a *Fantastic Four* or a *Spider-Man* adventure) is the light tone, the frivolity, that we find on the opening page of each book, when the credits are given. A list of typical credits follows:

*Extravagantly executed with ebullient erudition by Stan Lee and Jack Kirby. Inked by: Joe Sinnott. Lettered by: Sam Rosen.* (61 April FF)

*Contrived and crafted by the curiously creative, catastrophically compelling collaboration of Stan Lee and Jack Kirby. . . .* (62 May FF)

*Let Marveldom Cheer! Let humanity shout! Stan (the man) Lee and Jack (king) Kirby have bestowed another masterpiece upon mankind. Exotically embellished by Joe Sinnott, Laconically lettered by Artie Simek.* (73 April FF)

These credits establish a certain levity right away, so that the stories themselves take on a status somewhat removed from what might be called "high seriousness." What they do, more or less, is say to the reader, "Yes, we do a lot of kidding around, and that's how you should take the stories, but let's see what we can do with our super-heroes anyhow. . . ." That is, the credits show that readers aren't to take the stuff *too* seriously.

There is another reason for this horsing around, which has to do with the business of writing for comic books, an occupation which may

have considerable rewards financially but which has little status in the literary world. By clowning around a bit Stan Lee also protects himself from criticism by "stating" to the world that he recognizes what's going on, and doesn't take himself seriously.

Alliteration is one of the outstanding qualities of Lee's writing. That in itself shows that he sees the comic book as having a particular quality or status, which he reinforces by using language that is unnatural but remarkably intellectual. Alliteration involves the use of words with the same first letter or sound, such as the famous "pick a peck of pickled peppers." Many of the characters have alliterative names: Peter Parker, Betty Brant, Reed Richards, and Silver Surfer. Many of the titles use the same technique: *The Peerless Power of the Silver Surfer!* (55 Oct. FF): *The Tentacles and the Trap* (54 Nov. SM); *The Battle of the Baxter Building* (40 July FF); *By Ben Betrayed* (69 Dec. FF).

When fused with the right rhythms alliteration tends to create slogan-like phrases which stick in our memories. It is a favorite technique of advertising and politics: "Beat Benson with Burdick" was used to win a political campaign in North Dakota. Millions of Americans are implored to "Move up to Mercury" or "Buy Bonds."

*Alliteration is really a poetic device, and that is particularly important here, since there is no question in my mind but that the prose in Marvel comics is unusually poetic and at times quite lyrical.*

Silver Surfer episodes are always done in extremely poetical language, and this is combined with overt moralizing about the deficiencies and potentialities of man. Let's look at the way he speaks to see this. In the "Peerless Power" book, the adventure featuring him is called "When Strikes the Silver Surfer." The inversion of the language, together with the alliteration in the title, is a poetic technique. It has a much more lyrical quality than the normal order of words, "When The Silver Surfer Strikes." He describes himself in the following terms: *I, who have crested the currents of space . . . who have dodged the meteor swarms, and out-distanced the fastest comets, I must resign myself to this PRISON which men call earth . . . Because I dared give up the freedom of the universe to aid the hapless humans!*

## "NEVER HAS ANYONE FOUGHT SUCH MERCILESS FOES AS... "THE ENFORCERS!"

*But, I must have no regrets! Whatever destiny awaits me . . . I shall be true to my trust, though I am a stranger in a world I never made!* (55 Oct. FF p. 3). This description is, really, a self-important prose poem involving a meditation upon the human condition, the value of trust, and the mystery of destiny. It is spoken from the top of an enormous mountain peak, surrounded by other mountains and a vast landscape, as the Silver Surfer stands in an heroic pose peering out over the panorama. The whole scene is romantic and idyllic, as a nature-god (of sorts) ponders the future and what he might do to aid humanity. The Silver Surfer is a Christ-like figure. He gave up the freedom of the universe to come to the aid of mankind, and yet, despite all his fantastic powers, he does not know how to get around the greed and hatred which he sees in man. He is destined to eternal solitude, to being a stranger, and like Twain's *Mysterious Stranger*, his attempts to aid man, or force man to unite and realize his possibilities, are characterized by violence and destruction.

There is a vastness of scale here which is on the level of the epic, and, indeed, a closer look at the comics leads me to believe that they are modernized versions of the epic. In *A Glossary of Literary Terms* (p. 29) M. H. Abrams defines the epic as: "A long narrative poem on a serious subject, related in an elevated style, and centered about an heroic figure on whose actions depends to some degree the fate of a nation or a race. The 'traditional' or 'primary' epics were shaped from the legends that developed in an heroic age, when a nation was on the move and engaged in military conquest and expansion. In this group belong the *Iliad* and *Odyssey* of the Greek Homer, and the Anglo-Saxon *Beowulf*. The 'literary' or 'secondary' epics were written by sophisticated craftsmen in deliberate imitation of the earlier form. Of this kind is Virgil's Roman poem, the *Aeneid*, which in turn served as the chief model for Milton's literary epic, *Paradise Lost*."

Abrams says that the epic is an exceedingly difficult form which makes enormous demands on authors, and that consequently we have only a handful of unquestionably great epics. As he puts it, "It is certainly the most ambitious and most exacting of poetic types, making im-

HWAP!

UNGHH! THUNK!

BOP!

WHAM! SOK!

WHUMPH!!

WHEE

mense demands on a poet's knowledge, invention, and skill to sustain the scope, grandeur, and variety of a poem that tends to encompass the known world and a large portion of its learning" (pp. 29, 30). He lists certain characteristics of epics: a significant hero—of great importance; a world-wide (or even larger) scale; heroic actions and deeds in battle; the interest of the gods, who often take part in the action; and a ceremonial writing style, with a dignity proportionate to the subject. On the basis of this description of the epic I think we might claim that the comic book, with its superheroes and supervillains and its scope is often very close to the epic, and might be considered a kind of modernized epic, or a parody of the epic. The adventures of the Fantastic Four, who are "world-historical characters," whose actions are many times of importance to the whole world, often involve god-like individuals. We might call them "third-level" epics—since they make use of other materials and are not "high literature" as we commonly know it. The interesting thing is that in a literary form that is generally seen as just trash and seldom taken seriously, we find poetic language, philosophical speculation and the use of the epic and I have chosen to use this stylistic feature as a lead into especially of *The Fantastic Four,* really belongs in a section on narration, but the poetic and elevated style is an important characteristic of the epic and I have chosen to use this stylistic feature as a lead into the topic.

At the opposite extreme from lyrical and elevated language is the "language" used to create sound effects. There are an amazing collection of onomatopoetic creations used to suggest sounds. Onomatopoeia is a poetic device which uses words to simulate sounds, but the words in Marvel comics show a much greater range than in traditional poetic use. In addition the "words" used in comic strips can be given emphasis by being drawn in large letters, being brightly colored, or being given unusual shapes, as at the top of the page.

It can be seen that these sound effects play a rather dominant role in the panels which contain them. They spill over the boundaries of the panels, they are as large as some of the figures, and they are rather odd words. We find such creations as: "Krrash!", "Spkakk!", "Thoom!", and "Shoosh!" to name only a few. These terms represent an attempt

by the comic strips to transcend the limitations of the medium, just as the individual terms violate the borders of the panels. They also form a sub-language of sorts, a language of sound-effects. The acoustical terms give us an indication of exactly what kind of destruction is taking place or what kind of blows are landing. They have a cacophony that mirrors the chaos that is creating them—and also, by their size and shape, tell us the degree of emotion (sound) we are to experience. They function, that is, like a playwright's notes on how his play is to be produced—what the characters are to look like, how they are to feel, and what they are to experience. All of the actions take place in a special world of unreality and make-believe, which is carefully formed and which gives all the destruction and violence a particular status. This is the same kind of an effect we produce in a fairy tale when we say, "Once upon a time, long long ago, in a land very far away. . . ." This tells the listener how to feel about the story, regardless of what the story contains. Perhaps the best way to see the comic book is in theatrical terms. Instead of thinking of *Spider-Man* or *Fantastic Four* as comic books, think of them as illustrated plays. The dialogue is given in the balloons. The stage directions are given in the various inserts, and the thoughts (internal dialogue) of the characters are shown in balloons with fluffy edges. There are "conventions" to the comic book and a reader has to learn them in order to understand what is going on. In order to look at the language of Marvel comics without being affected by the graphic elements I will take part of an adventure and put it into the form of a play. That is, I will reduce it to the script from which it originally emerged. The following actors are involved in the adventure, which I am taking from the conclusion to issue number 10 of the *Spider-Man*:

J. JONAH JAMESON, publisher of *The Daily Bugle*
FREDERICK FOSWELL, writer on the staff of *The Daily Bugle*
SPIDER-MAN, otherwise known as Peter Parker
POLICEMEN
BETTY BRANT, Peter's girlfriend

The scene occurs at the end of an adventure in which the Spider-Man

Pop Culture/36

has defeated the Enforcers, a group of criminals, and broken up a crime syndicate. Only the leader of this group, a masked man known as the Big Man, has escaped. The scene takes place in the editorial offices of *The Daily Bugle*. Spider-Man is on a ledge outside the office and his presence is not known to the other characters. Jameson has just told Foswell to tear up an article he wrote on Spider-Man.

FOSWELL: Why? What's happened?

JAMESON: You fool! Haven't you heard the radio news bulletins?? The Enforcers have been CAPTURED! The crime syndicate is broken up! Only the BIG MAN has escaped! And the police are apt to find HIM before too long!

POLICEMAN: (entering door) : We've found him ALREADY Jameson!

JAMESON: Huh?

SPIDER-MAN: (to himself, from window ledge) : That clinches it! The high and mighty J. Jonah Jameson IS the big man himself! Although, in a way, I feel sorry! I never thought he was REALLY bad!

POLICEMAN: Don't try to sneak OUT of here, Foswell! We have the place surrounded! You might as well come along, peacefully!

JAMESON: Foswell?

SPIDER-MAN: (to himself) : Frederick Foswell?! But I thought it was Jonah?? How can little Foswell be the big man?

POLICEMAN: We found all the evidence we needed in your CAR, which we saw speeding away from the garage.

SECOND POLICEMAN: Pretty clever, Foswell—using special built-up shoes, an over-sized paded (sic) jacket, and a small amplifier to disguise your voice.

FOSWELL: (bitterly) : I'd have gotten away with it, TOO . . . if not for some crummy luck!

SPIDER-MAN: (to himself) : He ADMITS it! It IS Foswell! I never even suspected . . . some big brain I am! I not only have the proportionate STRENGTH of a spider—I'm just about as DUMB, too!

JAMESON: Even though YOU'RE the big man, Spider-Man WAS in league with you, wasn't he? ADMIT it! If he wasn't I'll be a laughing-stock AGAIN!

FOSWELL: BAH! I'll worry about it all the way to the jail!

(Later, after his office has emptied out . . .)

JAMESON soliloquy: Am I ALWAYS to be thwarted, embarrassed, frustrated by SPIDER-MAN?? I hate that costumed freak more than I've ever hated anyone before. I'll never be contented while he's free! All my life I've been interested in only one thing—making money! And yet, SPIDER-MAN risks his life day after day with no thought of reward! If a man like that is good—is a hero—then what am I?? I can never RESPECT myself while HE lives!

(Beam of light falls on Jameson)

Spider-Man represents everything that I'm NOT! He's brave, powerful and unselfish! The truth is, I ENVY him! I, J. Jonah Jameson—millionaire, leader—I'd give everything I own to be the *man* that HE is! (Italics added) But I can NEVER climb to his level! So all that remains for me is— to try to tear him down—because, heaven help me—I'm JEALOUS of him!

The rest of the page is devoted to introducing the next adventure which is to come the following month and is not of any particular concern to us.

It is obvious that there is more prose in comic books than we might expect. There are approximately 250 words on each of the two pages I have turned into script, which means that a twenty-two-page adventure would run about five thousand words, the size of a respectable short story. There are also 160 panels in this adventure, of which approximately one-fourth involve violence and mayhem. In one-eighth of the panels we find hand-to-hand fighting. All this violence takes place in three battle scenes, but under no circumstances could one say that the fighting or battling dominates the comic book. There is some

fighting, as we might expect in an adventure story, but I don't feel it is adequate to describe this story as "violence ridden," and I assume that this story is typical of the other Marvel comics.

There are a few intriguing aspects to the episode I have just recounted. The police are shown as intelligent and capable, which is somewhat different from the popular-culture stereotype of "the dumb cop." The role of the police in society is somewhat complicated: they are competent and intelligent, and yet there is a definite need for Spider-Man. This is because of the super-criminals, who function on a level beyond the capacities of ordinary people. Only the Spider-Man, with his super-powers, is able to contain the master criminals, and even he has a hard time doing this much of the time.

We even find Spider-Man being led astray, as, for example, with the identity of the Big Man. His life is complicated by a sick aunt and by his various romances. After all, he is a *teen* hero and has the same problems all teens have in American society; in addition he has the burden of his secret role as Spider-Man.

In the scene we are discussing we find a revelation by Jameson of the reason he continually persecutes Spider-Man, why he is always discrediting Spider-Man and trying to "tear him down." It is because Spider-Man, a *teen-age hero*, is more of a *man* than Jameson is. This is a classic study in the generation gap. Jameson, the older generation, has squandered his talents on "the ever-elusive goddess success," and though rich, recognizes that his life has been wasted and is meaningless. He is jealous of Spider-Man and because of this jealousy tries to destroy him. Of course we must realize that Jameson doesn't know the identity of Spider-Man, and assumes he is a man, but the young readers of the strip know, and the real message is that teenagers—young people—are "better" than old ones.

The significance of the teenager as "hero" has been discussed by a French sociologist, Edgar Morin. Morin claims that the main function of mass culture is no longer social control but "mythic," involving the creation of heroic figures. Daniel Bell, an eminent American scholar, explains Morin as follows ("Modernity and Mass Society," in *Paths of American Thought,* pp. 430, 431):

But contemporary mass culture . . . Morin has argued, goes beyond the age-old purpose of social control. Its essential function is "mythic"—to provide, since religion no longer can do so, a giant stage on which the new heroes and gods can be deployed. The authentic mythological hero, M. Morin claims, is the movie actor James Dean. In his brief explosive life, Dean fulfilled the classic requirements. He was an orphan, he ran away, he sought many different experiences ("labors"), and he became, at last, "what in the modern world incarnates the myth of a total life, a film star." Seeking the "absolute," unable to realize this in a woman's love, he found it instead in the ersatz absolute of "speed," and finally, meeting death in an auto crash, he gained immortality . . .

The distinctive feature of modern society, Morin argues, is that it has invented a new age of man—adolescence. In archaic societies, a boy was often violently initiated into manhood. In modern societies, youth refuses to be absorbed, and seeks, either through nihilism, delinquency, or beatnikism, to drop out of society. Rimbaud pointed the way with his nostalgia for childhood, his refusal to be "corrupted" by the adult world, by his desire "to live." In contemporary society, adolescents form their own world and elect their own heroes. With its "insatiable demand for personalities," mass culture today feeds upon this youth culture, Morin argues, and in doing so it has made heroes out of adolescent stars.

The center of gravity has shifted, at least in *Spider-Man*, to the adolescent, and we have an ironic reversal of roles. *The young person has become the model for the old person.* Spider-Man, an adolescent, incorporates values which are unquestionably more moral and decent than those of the "father-figure" J. Jonah Jameson, and many of the other adult characters in the various stories.

The use of a young person as hero or model is not new in American culture as we can see in *Huckleberry Finn*. Many sociologists and critics of American society have observed the same thing, and the idea that adults are either vicious or stupid is almost a cliché in contemporary American popular culture—especially in the situation comedies. But there is more realism in Marvel comics than in television situation

comedies, for the picture of young people that is shown is not always idealistic and heroic.

There is a great deal of bullying and unpleasant behavior to be seen—especially in the Spider-Man stories, which use the local high school as a frequent staging place. The teenagers portrayed in *Spider-Man* are shown to be rather shallow and stupid much of the time; the picture of the "typical teenager" is not a particularly attractive one. Peter Parker, a bookworm or "grind," is generally ostracized and ridiculed, especially in his earliest adventures. In the adventure from which the following page was taken (17, Oct. p. 3) "Flash," Peter Parker's nemesis, is establishing a Spider-Man fan club, but banishes Parker from it.

As one who doesn't fit in with other students, Parker is subjected to continual ridicule and insult. One of the girls in the in-crowd, Liz, likes Parker and defends him, but generally speaking the teenagers are, as she puts it, "cruel." Peter Parker's face and character have undergone continual change in the course of his career. He started off quite ugly, with glasses and sharp features. He has developed to a much more presentable young man in this adventure and as soon as the new artist, Johnny Romita, appears on the scene, Parker becomes what we would call a "swinger." He associates with pretty girls and rides a "horse" (motorcycle).

A later situation, in which two attractive girls are "fighting" over Peter, is quite far removed from early adventures of *Spider-Man*, and indicates a movement in the direction of a teen-age-romance-adventure kind of comic book. Parker now is a cool customer and can say, "LOOK, kiddies . . . This is all very FLATTERING, but I just remembered my aunt May has a new BOARDER, and I'd better see if everything's okay!" This kind of language is somewhat condescending and suggests that Parker has been socialized into rather typical American teenagerhood.

There are frequent passages in the various episodes in which Parker speculates on his guilt and his problems. His status in society is ambiguous: he is revered by some and hated by others—especially J. Jonah Jameson, who is continually trying to brand him a criminal and turn public opinion against him. These doubts, Parker's feelings of guilt and responsibility, are clearly shown in the adventure entitled "Spider-Man No More," in which Parker throws away his costume and renounces his identity as Spider-Man ('50, July, p. 7). This story also contains a flashback in which the murder of Uncle Ben is recounted, and a "recognition" scene in which Parker becomes aware of the burden which his great powers place on him. He realizes that "not acting" is a kind of acting—for had Spider-Man caught a fleeing criminal his Uncle Ben would have been alive. This scene (pp. 17-18) shows Parker dedicating himself to his role. He cannot allow innocent people to come to harm because he failed to act, and he decides to bear the burden, no matter how great the personal sacrifice. As he puts it, "It's all CRYSTAL CLEAR to me once more!" But I'm not so sure he does understand everything. He recognizes his guilt but I don't believe he understands that his actions as Spider-Man are to be also seen as an expiation for this guilt. Peter Parker cannot renounce Spider-Man because he must bear the burden of guilt, but at least he has some insight into his case and has a sense of obligation. In later adventures we are to find him still troubled, but that is his fate, and is, indeed, part of the human condition. In a later adventure Spider-Man has become an amnesiac. He wanders through the city, speculating about his identity, which is "lost." "All I know is . . ." he says, "I'm someone called SPIDER-MAN! Someone with NO YESTERDAYS—and with no TOMORROW" (S-M 56 Jan., 20). In many respects Spider-Man is a symbol of American youth—unsure of the past and with little optimism about the future. He has great abilities but cannot use them, is isolated from society at large (and forced, so to speak, to create his own "youth culture") and is disturbed by a profound sense of guilt. This is a heavy burden for anyone to bear. And for our young people, who are led to believe they have everything to hope for, yet are continually held down, shunted aside and deprived of a sense of possibility, it may be too much for them to take. The great irony is that, like Spider-Man, in many cases our young people are "heroes"—with no tomorrows.

## NOT GUILTY...?

Why do people act so violently? How can they be so vicious? I would answer by suggesting that many who resort to violence do so because they can justify it to themselves, and thus indulge in their passions and aggressions with impunity. We might call this the concept of "just hate"—*a means of liberating all the aggression and compensating for the frustrations we have within us, and not feeling guilt.* Such activity is often facilitated by mobs, which allow people to throw off the strictures of individual conscience and indulge in something akin to a blood lust.

If the situation is right, ordinary citizens—our neighbors, or the friendly policeman—can become cruel and violent, feel no guilt about inflicting pain and torture and become, *themselves,* brutalized. Stanley Milgram's famous "Eichmann experiment" showed that people will inflict alarmingly high levels of pain on other people *if* they can justify it to their consciences. In his experiment he told people that they were "helping science" and found, to his amazement, that they would inflict on victims shocks far greater than he (or other social scientists) would have imagined. The ordinary person, then, has a capacity for monstrous behavior if he can "liberate" himself from a conscience or a sense of guilt. An alarming number of people seem to have a capacity for hate if they can justify it to themselves, and can find a supportive environment.

In the last few years there has been what might be called a "comic craze." It started with the discovery that Batman was "camp." Batman's enormous success on television spread to the stage with Superman and led to such things as Jules Feiffer's anthology of "classic episodes" called *The Great Comic Book Heroes*. If the comics are ". . . a basic expression of American culture (and a) reflection of the predominant values in the life of the United States," as social psychologist William Albig put it in *Modern Public Opinion*, then perhaps we should take a better look at them than we have done in the past.

Because comic strips are popular in other countries, they furnish a very useful means for comparing attitudes and values. I made a study of some representative American and Italian comics (*fumetti* in Italian) and discovered that they reveal profoundly different attitudes toward the subject of authority.

For example, let us examine how the "military" is treated in American and Italian comics. The differences are so striking as to suggest that there are fundamental differences between the two cultures in general.

The great Italian "anti-military" comic hero is Marmittone (1928) by Bruno Angoletta. Like many of the earlier Italian comics, it is very simply drawn with rather stiff, wooden figures, plain backgrounds and dialogue in the form of rhymed verse (which appears in captions underneath the drawings). As in most comics, the dialogue isn't really necessary; it only adds details, although the rhyme and humor of the poetry are very amusing to children.

Marmittone is an extremely enthusiastic and zealous soldier who, as a result of bungling or bad luck, always ends up behind bars. Most of his adventures involve accidentally discomfiting officers or their friends and being reprimanded by being sent to the guardhouse. Marmittone is not rebellious at all. Indeed, he is just the opposite—he *respects authority figures*. He exhibits no desire to "cross" them, and if it were not for the fact that he is "jinxed" or perhaps even "doomed," he would be a model soldier. The only thing negative in the comic strip is that the hero, for whom we have affection and sympathy, ends up in prison—a dark, empty room into which a symbolic ray of light is always

seen filtering. It thus seems that *something* must be wrong if Marmittone, a good-willed hero, can end up in jail. But no direct attack is made on the officers; they are only obliquely ridiculed, and always at the *expense* of the hero.

In American "anti-military" comics such as Mort Walker's Beetle Bailey the attack is more direct. In this strip, currently one of the most popular in America, the common soldier consistently engages in the battle of wits with his superiors and generally emerges victorious. The sergeant and the captain in Beetle Bailey are both relatively sympathetic antagonists whose cupidity and stupidity endear them to the reader. It is the enlisted men who have the "upper hand" most of the time because they have the brains and because *authority is not seen as valid.* The sergeant is a good-natured, boisterous glutton, and the lieutenant is foolish and childish.

What's more, the ridicule is pictorial. In one episode, for example, the sergeant is seen coming through the "chow" line. He has a tray loaded with steaks, potatoes, salad, etc. "Wait," he says to the mess sergeant, "I don't have any celery." He also doesn't have any ice cream but the mess sergeant tells him there is no room on his tray and adds that there is "no coming through the line twice." The dilemma is solved by stuffing celery in the sergeant's ears and ice cream in his mouth. He thus "succeeds" but at the price of becoming a clown.

A contemporary Italian military strip dealing with the adventures of Gibernetta and Gedeone is somewhat closer to Beetle Bailey, though it retains the humorous poetry captions of Marmittone, and still has a reverential and respectful attitude toward authority. Rather than ending in prison as Marmittone always does, Gibernetta and Gedeone generally are awarded medals. The "fall guy" or the victim is the sergeant who blunders and suffers for it. Since receiving a medal is seen as a proper reward for the heroes, then the officers, the real authority figures, are still seen as *legitimate.* The sergeant, who is only instrumental in executing the wishes of the officers, is also, we must remember, an enlisted man who has risen—but he is still not a true authority figure.

Possibly the artist who draws the strip Cimpiani was influenced by

Walker, for his hero, Gibernetta, at times looks strikingly like Beetle. He has the same round head, his hair sticks out wildly from under his cap, his legs are thin and like toothpicks (this applies to all Cimpiani's characters); the only real difference is that you can see Gibernetta's eyes, whereas Beetle's are usually hidden under his hat.

Few of the "classic" Italian comics (such as Bonaventura, Bilbolbul, Pier Cloruro, or Pampurio) have the highly stylized, toothpick limbs and big feet that you find in Disney characters, such as Mickey Mouse. Both this kind of stylization and exaggeration and the realistic "draftsman" type *fumetti* (which aren't usually comic) are more or less American innovations, and fairly recent ones at that. Mickey Mouse dates from 1928 and "draftsman" style *fumetti* from Milton Caniff's Terry and the Pirates, 1934.

Mickey Mouse, known as Topolino in Italy, is probably the most important comic strip figure in Italy. He is the hero of at least one weekly magazine, *Topolino,* and a monthly, *Almanacco of Topolino.* Both magazines contain Donald Duck and other Disney characters and have some adventures that are written specifically for the Italian public. Almost 30 percent of the readers are between 16 and 34 years of age, which suggests that a good many of the fathers of children reading Topolino also read it. (The weekly edition has a circulation of 260,000 copies and *Almanacco* has a circulation of 140,000 copies per month.)

The Disney characters have a "supra-national"' appeal because they are simple animals and indulge in slapstick-filled cops-and-robber chases and activities amusing to all children. Donald Duck, Mickey Mouse, and their friends have also inspired a host of imitators so that there is now a comical cartoon character for almost every animal that exists.

But why should a mouse be so popular with children? Possibly because the mouse is a small, defenseless "household" creature that most children have seen, with whom they can empathize, and of whom they need not be afraid.

Historically, Mickey Mouse is a descendant of the mouse Ignatz in one of the greatest American comics, Krazy Kat, which flourished between

1911 and 1944 (until Herriman, its creator, died). But Krazy Kat was very different from Mickey Mouse. Ignatz Mouse was a decidedly *anti-social character*, constantly in rebellion against society, whereas Mickey Mouse is well adjusted, internalizes the values of his society, and is on the side of "law and order." He is comforting to children since he shows that submitting oneself to the values of a given order ends in well-being, rewards, and acceptance.

In the older "classics" of Italian and American comic repertoires, we find another interesting pair of "anti-social" animals, the American mule, Maud (1906), and the Italian goat, Barbacucco (1909).

Both animals are pitted against human beings—the goat butts people and the mule kicks them, but there is an important difference in the consequences. While Maud always ends up "victorious," the goat's actions always come to nothing. For example, he will butt a tree in which a boy and a girl are sitting and the fruit will fall down, which they then eat. On the other hand, all attempts to "tame" Maud, the ornery mule, are useless and people who try are most always defeated, though they might have momentary and temporary successes.

Maud is a rebel who succeeds; Barbacucco is a rebel who does not, and perhaps, in a strange way, they mirror two different attitudes: the American type of self-sufficient individualism and the Italian idea that somehow the "given order of society" is too strong to be bucked, that things are "fated." Whether the fates are smiling or not is beside the point, for if things are ultimately fated, individual initiative and efforts are of no great importance—"whatever will be will be."

Probably the best example of this reliance "on the gods" is the famous Italian comic hero, Bonaventura, who started amusing children in 1917. Graphically, Bonaventura is typically "old school" Italian—the figures are stiff and crudely drawn, little attention is paid to landscape (which is highly stylized and greatly over-simplified), there is not much expression on the faces of the characters, there is much fantasy, and the dialogue is given in rhymed verse captions.

Things do not *always* turn out well for Bonaventura (which means "good adventures" or "good luck"). When he instigates actions and activities—such as trying to drive a car or trying to become a social lion—things turn out badly for him and he generally retreats and goes back to simpler ways and more secure activities. It is only by chance (even the malicious acts of his nemeses are chance events) that potential "disasters" turn out well for him, and he earns his *milione* (fortune). Thus, at the end of an episode in which Bonaventura tries to drive automobiles, with calamitous results, he decides that from now on he will walk; or at the end of an adventure in which he tries to "enter society," he decides that society is full of delusions and that he will remain with his sweet and good family. For reasons such as these, I think we can call Bonaventura a decidedly *conservative* character, or one who embodies a conservative outlook toward experience. This, in turn, suggests that Bonaventura isn't as optimistic a strip as is commonly believed in Italy. Bonaventura's "rebellions" against the more cloying aspects of family life or the limitations of being a pedestrian end in defeat. And even when he gets his *milione* it is generally the result of a freak occurrence; it is always rather "miraculous." Individual initiative is played down and luck is all; the best of all possible rewards is seen as money. Bonaventura is a materialist who emphasizes for readers that the only way to become a success in the world is through a miracle—not a particularly hopeful outlook.

There are several other comparisons between American and Italian comics that suggest differences in attitudes toward royalty and aristocracies and the treatment of the "mischievous" child. Soglow's "The Little King," which started appearing in 1934, is very close to the classical Italian comic in style, but far different in attitude. The king, a fat dwarf who has a big mustache, always wears his crown and generally an ermine robe. But he is humanized. He fetches the milk in the morning, he rushes to bargain clearances in department stores, and is generally shown to be "just like anyone else." He is made into a good democrat, and there is no suggestion of any divinity "that doth hedge a king." Indeed, both the title of the strip, "The Little King," and the fact that he is mute, indicate this. Rubino's "Lola and Lalla" is much different. Here, Lola, the daughter of a rich man (we have an aristocracy of wealth here), is always elaborately dressed and quite vicious toward Lalla, her social inferior. Lalla is always shown in "modest but clean" clothing, decidedly inferior to that of Lola. As a result of being pushed around by Lola, however, she ends up with more beautiful clothing. Generally this is accomplished by having some sticky substance fall on Lalla to which flower blossoms become attached.

Here the aristocracy, as represented by Lola, is seen as vicious and brutal, repulsing any attempt by the common people (Lalla) to be friendly or to gain recognition. Social class is shown by clothing, as in "The Little King." But whereas the king is warm and very human, as we might expect from a democratic American king, the European aristocracy is demonic and insists that the people "know their place." Social mobility is impossible and any attempts at it are repulsed. Even Lola's dog, conventionally a friendly animal, is shown as nasty and cold, corrupted, we imagine, by his relationship with Lola and the "upper classes."

A similar attitude in Italian comics deals with "naughty" children. That is, in many of the episodes the mischievous child is caught and punished; the price of rebellion is a spanking or some kind of humiliation. This is different from many American comics, in which the child often succeeds.

Take, for example, Rubino's remarkable strips Pierino and Quadratino, who appeared from 1909 on. Pierino is a little boy who is always trying to get rid of his doll, but never succeeds. He buries it, he gives it away, he throws it down the chimney—but no matter, it keeps coming back. Generally in the last panel the same shaft of light that fell on Marmittone in jail now falls on Pierino, although in this case the ray of light probably symbolizes internalized conscience rather than socially "objectionable" activities.

Quadratino is a boy whose head is a cube. His escapades generally result in his head getting changed in shape, so that the fact that he has committed "crimes" becomes visible. There is much distortion in the strip and a good deal of plane geometry. But the moral of Quadratino (and of Pierino) is that bad boys always get caught or, in more general terms, *rebellion against properly constituted authority is perilous and futile.*

It might be objected that Hans and Fritz, the Katzenjammer Kids, also usually end up being punished, and this is true. But there is an important difference to be noted between the endings in the Katzenjammer Kids and in Rubino's strips. Generally, the pranks of Hans and Fritz are successful and cause a great deal of discomfort to the adults against whom they are directed. Thus, the pranks are successful as pranks. It is only the fact that adults, having a monopoly on force, can get their revenge—and do so—that pales the victories of the kids (and tans their hides).

Let me summarize the underlying psychological and social attitudes in these comics and which I am hypothesizing might be broadly accepted cultural values:

### ITALIAN COMICS

| Character | Attitude to Authority |
|---|---|
| Marmittone (1928-1953) | respects constituted authority, zealous, but jinxed |
| Gibernetta (contemporary) | respects authority |
| Barbacucco (1910-1924) | unsuccessful in his rebellion against people |
| Bonaventura (1917-1965) | bad luck turns out miraculously for the best, conservative approach to experience |
| Lola and Lalla (1910-1913) | interaction between classes impossible, upper classes seen as demonic |
| Quadratino (1910) | rebellion against authority |
| Pierino (1909) | (adult world) seen as futile |

### AMERICAN COMICS

| Character | Attitude to Authority |
|---|---|
| Beetle Bailey (1953-present) | authority not recognized as valid |
| Mickey Mouse (1928-present) | values of the given order are valid |
| Ignatz Mouse (1913-1944) | anti-social and rebellious |
| Maud (1906) | anti-social and rebellious (successfully) |
| Little King (1934-present) | democratic "King"—no different from anyone else |
| Katzenjammer Kids (1898-present) | rebellion against adult world successful in short run, but often has bad consequences |

These Italian comics reflect a basically conservative approach toward experience and society. Authority is generally portrayed as valid and rebellion against it as futile. Social mobility must depend on miracles in a rigid and hierarchical society in which all attempts to climb are brusquely repulsed.

The American comics described here suggested, on the other hand, an irreverential approach toward authority. Authority is often invalid, and not necessarily worthy of respect. So there is much more anti-social and rebellious activity, which is seen as possibly successful. Mickey Mouse is the only conformist of the group; but then Mickey, as I have already pointed out, is also very popular in Italy.

These conclusions are, of course, tentative—they have been drawn from a rather limited reading of a rather small group of comics. On the other hand, these comics cover a wide range in time and concept, and some of them can rightly be considered to be classics. Moreover, I did not choose them because they dealt with authority, but merely tried to compare comics that were similar in time and subject (for instance, Maud and Barbacucco). I found that with a number of important strip characters the outstanding difference revolved around the way authority was treated.

It is, I think, much more than coincidence that these values found in the comic strips parallel closely what social scientists and skilled observers have had to say for a long time about the different attitudes toward authority in the United States and other countries. For example, de Tocqueville said in *Democracy in America*:
To the European, a public officer represents a superior force: to an American, he represents a right. In America, then, it may be said that no one renders obedience to man, but to justice and law. If the opinion which the citizen entertains of himself is exaggerated, it is at least salutary; he unhesitatingly confides in his own powers, which appear to him to be all-sufficient.

Recently, Glen H. Elder, Jr., studied family authoritarianism in five countries and found that Italy was the most authoritarian country and America the least authoritarian one. This would suggest, then, that comics accurately reflect values and are worthy of more serious attention.

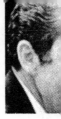

## THE POLITICS OF WRESTLING

In America we have long believed that because we are not a militaristic nation (or were not), we are also not a violent people. *The reason we aren't militaristic is that we don't respect authority, not that we don't believe in violence,* and, in fact, our feelings about authority contribute to our sanctioning of violence. For anyone who has doubts about the amount of violence pervading American society, a glance at the television screen or at the daily newspaper provides ample evidence that, for one reason or another, this is a violent society.

History shows that we achieved independence by violence, expanded by violence, preserved the union by violence and protected our freedom by violence. We have been engaged in wars for the past half-century, and have been fighting one in Vietnam which most Americans believe is a tragic mistake, a war which directed our attention away from our own problems in America and which led to a certain degree of brutalization of our society. In the past, however, violence has paid off handsomely and has become a basic value, permeating our culture.

As a starting place for reflection on this situation, I suggest we look at a rather commonplace aspect of American life—wrestling, as it is seen on television—to see how it helps reinforce our commitment to violence. One of my assumptions is that we learn a great deal outside of the classroom and, in fact, what we learn in everyday life is possibly more important than what we learn from school. After all, we don't go to school until we are five or six, we spend only a few hours in school, and values tend to be "set" before we ever put foot in the classroom. The average American child spends more time watching television than he spends in the classroom, so there is great reason to suspect that television has a significant impact upon the socialization of American children.

Let's examine a typical television wrestling match. What we see, I might add, both reflects American values and reinforces them—it is a two-way process. What we must do, however, is look at television wrestling as something other than an "exhibition" between two actor-athletes. There is a "politics" to wrestling and *what* we learn from examining it is that our entertainments can inform our view of life and

in a sense indirectly affect a number of phenomena in American life: paramilitary armies, mass murders, our love of contact sports, and the like.

We find the following participants in a typical match: a referee, a hero and a villain. The referee, "appointed by the state athletic commission," is stupid, weak and dangerous. He is always duped by the villain and actually gets in the way of the hero.

The hero is forced to resort to extra-legal acts to offset the advantages gained by the villain's dirty tactics—punches, eye gouging, judo "cuts," biting, strangling, kicks to the stomach, back, head, etc. Typically the hero uses his fists and punches the villain, though when sufficiently angered it is considered acceptable to give the villain some of his own medicine.

Very often, I might add, the villain wins: there is no guarantee of the triumph of the morally superior, and there are many "slaughters," in which a "clean" wrestler of 230 pounds is matched with a villain weighing 260 or 300 pounds, and is massacred. The overmatched hero may, on occasion, get in a few blows, but generally he takes all kinds of abuse and ends up on the mat unable to move. The fate of the various wrestlers depends upon their image and charisma. Certain small wrestlers are "winners" and invariably triumph due to their "speed," supposedly Herculean strength, or some other dynamic attribute. Geographic location also is a factor. Mexican wrestlers tend to be dirty villains in Los Angeles and clean heroes in San Francisco; thanks to cultural lag, "Germans" are still usually villains. Blacks are often heroes, especially if they were famous football players.

All of the hokum in television wrestling is accompanied by incredible excitement on the part of the studio audience, who identify with the heroes, scream at the villains, and seem to obtain a genuine catharsis. It is always amusing to see gray-haired grandmotherly types screaming "break his arm" or "kill him," as they encourage the heroes. The people who attend and most who watch wrestling matches are supposed to be working class and lower-middle class for the most part. You can tell this from the advertisements on television during the matches: vitamin tonics, low-priced used cars, cold remedies, etc. Other classes have other amusements, some of which employ different kinds of violence.

If we move from the realm of personalities to that of institutions and social forces, we find that certain culturally significant things take place. It is hard to see a pattern because the various "freak" characters such as Haystacks Calhoun and his like do tend to obscure the matter, but certain patterns emerge which speak to our *unconscious*. For a graphic presentation of what I am talking about, examine the chart on *The Dynamics of Wrestling,* which follows. This chart deals with the activity of the participant in the wrestling match, the social and cultural significance of each participant, and the meaning of his actions.

### THE DYNAMICS OF WRESTLING

| Participant in Match | Symbolically Represents | Action |
|---|---|---|
| Referee | Authority of State | Blunders, inadvertently helps villain, hurts hero. Weak. Stupid. |
| Villain | Evil Forces in Society | Dupes state, cheats, lies, uses power of state against hero and the good. |
| Hero | Good Forces in Society | Hurt by state's interference, must use extra-legal acts to save self. |

What this chart shows, in abbreviated form, can be explained as follows:

1. The authority and validity of the state, or government, are voided. The representative of the state, the referee, is, in effect, a fool and rather than helping the hero he generally hurts him. This leads to the notion that the state is our enemy, even when it is trying to help us.

In the matches when the hero has been provoked by the villain and threatens him, the referee usually prevents the hero from hitting the villain. In essence the state only acknowledges for the record what has happened as antagonists who are outside its control contest for power and success.

2. Issues become oversimplified and we find what is called "the two-valued orientation"—the primeval battle between the hero (who is all good) and the villain (who is all bad). We find no intermediate ground: everything is either good or evil. We find blacks or whites, and no grays, ethically speaking. Political sociologists have identified this simplistic kind of thinking as being typical of the working classes, and it is now associated with the "hard hat" phenomenon in American political life. The implications of the two-valued orientation are that evil, since it is "absolute evil," must be eliminated by any means possible, which leads directly into the politics of extremism.

3. The hero, to protect himself from the villain, must resort to extra-legal activities. He is forced into the tragic matches and after provocation, the hero usually adopts some of the vicious tactics of the villain, except that he does so only as a response to aggression. This is a typically American stance, just a few steps removed from the "chip on the shoulder" game of children. The important point is that lawlessness is sanctioned in the name of justice, and, in fact, encouraged because of the unregenerate nature of the villain.

4. The actions of the hero, namely the use of violence, reinforce the notion that violence is an efficacious way of solving problems. After all, the hero saved himself by resorting to violence. All of wrestling is permeated by violence—the violence of the wrestlers and the violent responses of the viewers, and it is quite likely that one of the worst effects of watching wrestling on the unconscious is that we get the idea that violence is, really, the *only* means of solving problems, when you get right down to it! This ultimately leads to anarchy, a situation in which there is no legitimate rule, just chaos and violence. The state, which is traditionally defined as that which has a monopoly on the legitimate use of violence within a given area, is replaced by multitudes of violent factions, each contesting its own interests. And given the high incidence of triumph by the forces of evil, the "villains," in

the wrestling matches, it is not a hopeful situation. Everything reduces itself to individual "initiative" and strength, and one is left with the image of a society in which life is "nasty, brutal, and short." Our extracurricular political education, as it is furthered by such things as wrestling matches, detective stories, and westerns, seems to me to be inherently dangerous and anti-social. People cannot help but be affected by such entertainment—even if they are aware that the action and theatricality of the matches are fake. And since they watch these things every week, the force of incremental repetition is at work, and the experiences and the violence become qualitatively more important as the quantity of watching increases.

Wrestling, then, is a good example of the political science of the everyday man—or, at least, certain tendencies in his political thought. It is a reflection, actually, of the Jeffersonian legacy of the negative state and of atomic individualism, which postulates that each individual has his destiny completely in his own hands (or fists) and must look out for himself. In recent years wrestling has been eclipsed by the development of roller derby, a sport with the same cultural dynamics but even more violence. It features teams of men or women who skate around an oval track and try to score points by lapping the field. It offers many opportunities for violence—for tripping skaters, for knocking them off the track, for elbowing them in the stomach (euphemistically called a "block")—and it has created many "heroes" who have become celebrities on account of their ability to provoke fights, use dirty tactics and create chaos. All of this goes on as the skaters flash around and around the track, at great speed. But being a team activity, it does not reflect the underlying beliefs about man and politics as well as wrestling.

## BASEBALL IS A BORE

Baseball has become a big bore to me. I never thought I'd ever say that. I lived in Boston in 1946 when Thumping Theodore Williams (The Splendid Splinter) was performing heroics, when the Red Sox had the likes of Bobby Doerr, Dom DiMaggio, Rudy York and some five or six .300 hitters in the lineup. Those days we followed baseball with passion, and our hearts skipped a few beats when the scores came over the radio.

But sometime during the past several decades something happened. Baseball didn't seem to matter anymore. It wasn't because there were so many mediocrities playing. (The quality has deteriorated so much that good players are now stars and stars are superstars.) And it isn't due to the inanities of the owners, wandering with their teams from city to city in search of patrons.

Football and baseball obviously have different "personalities" and what I suggest is that our character has changed. These changes line up with the values we find in football.

Baseball became irrelevant. Football now reflects the basic, underlying cultural dynamics of contemporary America. Football is urban, it uses "educated" players, it is complex, specialized, violent and sexy. In football every second counts, as it does in America, where "time is money." And football has another important virtue—it televises well. In all these respects it reflects values and impulses that are now dominant. It is now even *MORE* American than baseball.

Baseball is essentially pastoral. It is an anachronistic holdover from the nineteenth century. It is simple, mechanical, has no body contact to speak of, is chaste, unconcerned about time, and dull. Some games can take five hours, and in a good pitcher's duel you can see a whole game with hardly a hit. Baseball's dilemma is that at its best technically it is at its worst from a spectator's point of view.

In a sense you can say that baseball has become dull because we have become "hopped up." In an urban, competitive, conformist society we live under pressure and we like our sports to have pressure in them. Football provides us with an opportunity to let off steam, to get rid of tensions, to have what is called a "catharsis." Baseball's excitement is rare and doesn't pervade the game the way it does in football. Except, perhaps, in the World Series, there is no such thing as an "upset" in baseball as there is in football. And since football games are played but once a week, each one is qualitatively more important. There is also a certain amount of spectacle in football—the bands, the half-time shows, the pretty cheerleaders, and even the dress of the spectators. In comparison baseball is austere and ascetic.

To see these differences more graphically, look at the chart which compares the two sports:

| FOOTBALL | BASEBALL |
| --- | --- |
| Urban | Pastoral |
| "Educated" Players | Country Boys |
| Time Precious | Time No Factor |
| Specialized | Not Specialized |
| Body Contact | Little Contact |
| Sexual | Chaste |
| Team Effort | Individualistic |
| Upsets Critical | No Upsets |
| Vicarious Excitement | Relaxation |
| Weekly | Daily |

# FIVE WAYS OF LOOKING AT A FOOTBALL COACH
## or AGONY ON THE SIDELINES

Thanks to the miracle of television (which has made football—professional and college—so much a part of the American way of life) we are treated from time to time to real-life dramas of great passion and poignancy. I am speaking of the occasional close-up shots we are given of professional football coaches pacing nervously along the sidelines, giving frantic orders to various lesser coaches and other minions. When their teams are doing poorly, their agonies tear at the heartstrings. Although what I have to say covers all coaches, I will concentrate on the professional "play-for-pay" coaches, with their crews of all-American seasoned veterans, whose errors and foibles cannot be credited to lack of experience or youthful indiscretion.

There are, I believe, five basic ways of looking at the football coach as far as his "function" and the way he is presented by sportswriters to the general public is concerned. Furthermore, coaches pass from one "identity" to another, eventually, except for a few geniuses who do not experience the agony along the sidelines.

The first way a coach is presented, usually when he is newly hired or if he is particularly successful, is as what I call the "expert-technocrat." He is characterized as the man who has mastered the intricacies of professional football—as an apprentice for some guru coach—and will make the team into a formidable organization and cause *other* coaches agony on the sidelines. Thus, if one has been an assistant coach for Vince Lombardi it is assumed that some of the genius has rubbed off.

His second characterization is as the "tyrant-torturer," putting his charges through their paces: firing paunchy veterans (who at 35 are superannuated) and making the players do horrible exercises to get them in condition. Before the football season starts there are usually TV film clips showing training camps with players bridging on their necks and ramming themselves into bizarre contraptions.

Next comes the manifestation of coach as "impotent father." He must stand idly by at the sidelines as his players (sons) make all kinds of stupid errors he has warned them against and taught them how to avoid. In football, as in life, you can only take your players so far.

The rest is up to them—and often in football, as in life, people make lots of mistakes. A coach can be an "impotent father" and still win, for his charges may make errors but they also may "find" themselves, and if they do so enough times, especially around their opponent's goal line, the agony will not be too great.

*All coaches have these three identities: expert-technocrat, tyrant-torturer and impotent father.* But all coaches do not take on the next, and unredeemable, identity—that of the "suffering servant." In this identity he is the scapegoat, who takes on himself all the agony of the community so as to lessen the burden for everyone else. And the crowds discharge all their pent-up feelings on him, as soon as it is evident that his role is that of suffering servant and not expert-technocrat. In this respect football is a kind of community ritual which takes care of certain social needs: the release of hostility and aggression, association with a "winner," and sacrifice of the "suffering servant," the willing (?) victim.

As you watch the coaches pace nervously back and forth along the sidelines, especially during close games, you cannot help but feel pity for them. As the tension mounts they, more than anyone else, suffer a thousand tortures—even in cases in which their team comes from behind and wins. Their faces often express the nameless terror they feel —and it is not acting, as in plays. It is the real thing.

Eventually, in a parody of the Roman gladiatorial contests, the crowds demand losing coaches be ousted. For the suffering of the "suffering servant" no longer is effective in absorbing the social pain and a new coach is required: either to suffer or make fans loyal to other teams suffer. "Goodbye Allie Goodbye," chanted the crowds in New York, and that was the end of Allie Sherman. He dared to lose—and in football, more than any other game, it is the coach who loses as much as the players. Football is a game of decision-making, and the "suffering servant" has made the wrong decisions.

For him there remains the last step—being fired, becoming an *ex-coach*. The cycle has run out, and from here there are three possibilities. He may retire for good, he may get a job as an assistant coach on some other team, or he may get another position as head coach (if he can) so that the cycle begins again. Somebody else may think he is an "expert—technocrat" and give him another chance.

Naturally, "suffering servants" are paid well—often as much as $50,000 a year, or close to $3,000 a game in some cases. That is cheap for the agony they have to bear: blocked punts, fumbles on their own ten-yard line, dropped passes, touchdowns called back because of penalties, interceptions, a tide of other woes too numerous to mention, including the enmity of the fans—in whom love and admiration have turned to fanatical revulsion. On a per capita basis it is also quite reasonable and it is no accident that the popularity of football on television (and its ability to provide us with relief via "suffering servants") has coincided with our time of troubles: wars, social discontent, and student rebellions.

## FILL IN THE NAME OF YOUR FAVORITE
## GREASY (PLASTIC) SPOON ...

_____ offers the hamburger without
qualities for the man without qualities. It must
be seen as more than a gaudy, vulgar oasis of
tasteless ground meat, a fountain of sweet,
syrupy malted milks in a big parking lot, which
caters to insolvent students, and snack seekers.
_____ is not just a hamburger joint—
it is America, or rather, it is the supreme triumph of all that is insane in American life.
At _____ there is no human touch ...
just little packets of hamburgers, sacks of fried
potatoes. Everything is packed in bags to be
thrown away. Is there any pleasure connected
with eating a _____ hamburger? Does
one find it enjoyable? I think not! The only
relief you have is that it didn't cost fifty cents or
even forty-nine cents.

But we do purchase our _____ hamburger at great cost. We cannot have it rare or
well done, we cannot have it without "the
works," for that would destroy its integrity. No!
We get the great national hamburger—prepared to hamburgize the masses—which forces
us to sacrifice our individuality, our gastronomic
identity, for a few pennies. Instead of the
hamburger being prepared for _our_ tastes, we
are forced to adapt ourselves to it; we must
mold ourselves to _its_ taste. The triumph of
_____ ism is the death of individualism
and the eating of a _____ hamburger
is the next thing to a death wish. (A
_____ hamburger reminds you how
very mortal you are, how you too will be
thrown away some day in the metal equivalent
of a paper bag.)

# THE RELIGIOUS FACTOR IN FOOTBALL

When news came that the pro football's strike of 1970 was settled, it was a source of great relief for millions of fans. For a while it looked as if there would be no season. Sports pundits were predicting a season of re-runs, replays, computer games and other absurdities, and football owners and television networks were going crazy, having "withdrawal of revenue" nightmares. But finally an accommodation was reached and the pros were to play for us again.

This great scare phenomenon is extremely interesting. Since the fans would still have had college football to watch, they would not have been deprived of all television football. The reason the threatened strike seemed calamitous, I think, is that professional football is more than a mere sport—it is a religion of sorts which expresses a philosophy that orients viewers to the world and explains how it "runs." College football, in this respect, is like a lay church. It functions the same way, but without a professional clergy it is not quite as satisfying.

When we say, for example, that a football team is finally "putting it all together," we are suggesting that it is functioning well. But if you take the phrase in a philosophical manner we are asserting that somehow the world makes sense. Football fans do not agree with existentialists who argue that life is absurd and the world meaningless. To the football fan the idea of grown men knocking themselves out chasing an inflated oval (the heresy of reductionism is implicit in this description of the game) is not at all silly or absurd.

The tackling and body-contact tell us that while the world is full of conflicts and obstacles, we can often overcome them. One important aspect of the game is that there is stratification—with some jobs being more glamorous than others. The backfield is the aristocracy and the line is the peasantry. Linemen are seldom holdouts in salary disputes, the moral equivalent of the prodigal son.

From the instant replays we get the idea that time is somehow "recoverable," that it can be repeated and is not lost once it passes. (This suggests immortality.) The past keeps on repeating itself. Football on television is not very far removed from esoteric films such as *Last Year at Marienbad*.

There can be little question that all kinds of beliefs and actions traditionally associated with religion can now be found, in a secularized and transformed nature, in professional football. The names of the teams are *totems* which are meant to have a magical significance, and often associate the team with strong beasts. The game is highly formalized and structured, much like a church service, with many rituals and observances.

Here are some other parallels between modern football and religion:

| PROFESSIONAL FOOTBALL | RELIGION |
|---|---|
| Superstars | Saints |
| Sunday Game | Sunday Service |
| Ticket | Offering |
| The Great Merger | Ecumenical Movements |
| Complicated Plays | Theology |
| Player on Way to Superbowl | Knight in Search of Holy Grail |

Men seem to have some kind of a need for myth, ceremony, and ritual, which football supplies in place of organized religion. And as religion "demythologizes" and becomes more and more "un-mysterious," football becomes more mysterious and fantastic—with wildly complicated attacks and formations that function the way theology and doctrine do for religion. Is football taking the place of organized religion, especially Christianity, in America (since football is an American sport and America is essentially a Christian country)? America has a genius for inventing religions. There are probably more religions in southern California, for example, than in the rest of the world. Is it not possible, then, that football is one also, though we may not be aware of it as such?

## WHEN VIOLENCE IS GOLDEN ...

In a memorable passage in *Dick Tracy*, in a scene just before he vaporizes the arch-villain "Intro" (a monster we never meet), Tracy says, *"VIOLENCE IS GOLDEN WHEN IT IS USED TO PUT DOWN EVIL."* Over fifty million people read this, and I would venture to say most of them believed it. After all, as we have been told, "Violence is as American as apple pie" . . . or was it "cherry pie"?

The statistics about violence are horrendous: some 8,000 Americans were shot last year, as compared to a few dozen in Japan and the Netherlands, for example. And violence pervades American culture, from the novels of Faulkner to the television screens to the movies to the comics. It is forever everywhere. As a result of the assassinations of Martin Luther King and Robert Kennedy, people have started thinking about violence and taking it more seriously. An advisory committee appointed by the Surgeon General has investigated television and concluded that televised violence is connected with aggressive behavior.

We are only now beginning to realize how much violence informs our culture, though we can't be sure just where the roots of this violence are, what are its cause and effect. It is likely that violence is tied to our famous (or notorious) success ethic. Certain sociologists have suggested that this success drive, which is so powerful in the U. S., is the primary motivation behind our gangsters. They must succeed, at all costs, and if they can't do it within the law, they do it outside of it. Success is also behind our use of violence; we feel we must achieve whatever it is we desire, and if we are frustrated, we take recourse in violence. We legitimatize the use of violence, whether in putting down evil, or putting down anyone who happens to stand in our way.

This intoxication with violence is reinforced by our mass media. Most of our culture heroes, from Popeye and Superman to our cowboys, detectives and secret agents, are men of violence. They may be using violence to put down evil, but whatever the case, they are violent. And from them *we get the idea that violence is legitimate given the right situation,* and we make situations right and violence acceptable quite easily.

Some media experts have suggested that the news from the Vietnam war also creates an atmosphere of violence. This is our first television war, in which you can see actual fighting and dead bodies which are really dead. The air is full of body counts and bomb tonnages. The question, however, is this: are we violent because we are in Vietnam or are we in Vietnam because we are violent? I would say the latter, but since violence feeds upon itself, for all practical purposes it doesn't make any difference.

We are in Vietnam because of our sense of *mission*, because we are positive that we have the right answers when it comes to governing nations—though we are there, we say, to protect democracy and insure self-determination. Because we are sure we are right, our violence becomes, in Tracy's words, "golden." Thus we face the ironic situation that a people who think of themselves as innocent, easygoing, and good-natured find themselves in a bloody and horrible war 10,000 miles from their shores and their society racked by violence and murder. And the violence in Vietnam and the violence at home nourish each other and grow more monstrous with each day. America is quickly becoming an armed camp just like Vietnam.

What is particularly terrifying is that violence has even become comic. There is an element of the physical in much comedy—in slapstick, for example, when we push a lemon meringue pie in somebody's face, but the aggression is masked and relatively minor. However, lately violence has been used for creating comedy with devastating effect. Take, for example, the film *The President's Analyst,* a satire on spy stories. It started off with a brutal and unnecessary murder, in terms of the plot line, and moved on to bigger, better, and more hilarious murders. There was one scene in which a housewife, skilled in karate, fought off a group of secret agents, while her husband, an accountant, shot them down with devastating accuracy. In another scene, a group of secret agents murdered each other in a linear progression, with poison arrows, pitchforks, and the like.

I would estimate that no fewer than fifty people were killed in that film, though most of them were shot in a "battle" between spies and the telephone company. All this in a comedy. Perhaps our rec-

ognition that all of this murder and mayhem is make-believe and a satire on regular spy stories made the terror acceptable. Still, it must have some kind of an effect—visceral, if nothing else. From that movie we could go on to sales *riots* with *slashed* prices, gas "wars," getting "bombed," going to "blasts," "blowing up," being "torpedoed," and so forth. And the coaches' familiar exhortation to players, especially in basketball, to "get physical," which really means "play rough." My point is that the imagery of violence and terror pervades our society. The term violence is very close to *violate*, and this gives us an important insight. You only use violence—force and raw power (whether it be an army or a gun) —when you are absolutely positive that you are right and therefore can legitimately violate the rights of another person (or country) to space or dignity or life or liberty. The power of life and death has traditionally been reserved for the gods. Those who kill people whether physically or by destroying their dignity must be convinced that they are gods or the servants of gods. And the distinction quickly fades.

## SOME ENCHANTED EVENING
## YOU WILL FIND IT'S ALL IN THE GAME

I remember when *South Pacific* opened on Broadway. All the juke boxes suddenly had Ezio Pinza's glorious voice blaring forth with "Some Enchanted Evening," a wonderful tune which, among other things, explains how people fall in love. What happens, the song tells us, is that "you will see a stranger across a crowded room" and zingggg—you will fall in love. When this happens you must "rush to her side and make her your own," otherwise "all through your life you will dream on alone."

This is what love is like, according to "Some Enchanted Evening" and, for that matter, most love songs, including some of our contemporary rock songs. But this isn't the way people fall in love in real life.

According to Peter L. Berger, in *Invitation to Sociology* (p. 35):

*In Western countries, and especially in America, it is assumed that men and women marry because they are in love. There is a broadly based popular mythology about the character of love as a violent, irresistible emotion that strikes where it will, a mystery that is the goal of most young people and often of the not-so-young as well. As soon as one investigates, however, which people actually marry each other, one finds that the lightning-shaft of Cupid seems to be guided rather strongly within very definite channels of class, income, education, racial and religious background . . . The suspicion begins to dawn on one that, most of the time, it is not so much the emotion of love that creates a certain kind of relationship, but that carefully predefined and often planned relationships eventually generate the desired emotion. In other words, when certain conditions are met or have been constructed, one allows oneself "to fall in love."*

The point, then, is that we really don't (usually) fall in love some enchanted evening. But, rather, when we deem the conditions acceptable we allow ourselves to be overcome by emotion and everything else connected with falling in love. ("Love," said a wit, "is an island of emotion surrounded by a sea of expenses.")

Few sociologists are song writers, and the reality of how people fall in love does not lend itself to songs as easily as does the myth, so millions of people keep looking around in crowded rooms and waiting for lightning to strike.

We must recognize that popular music plays a very important role in socializing people—in teaching them something about how to live and love. And there are songs and styles of music for all tastes—pop, rock, folk, jazz, country western, blues, protest music, anthems, football rousers, as well as various combinations of these styles.

I remember I was playing the Beatles' "Revolution" when, by a curious coincidence, my class was invaded by revolutionaries in the famous San Francisco State College strike of the late sixties. (The revolutionaries, incidentally, listened to the song, but were "not amused," perhaps because "revolution" is really an anti-revolutionary song.) Popular songs tell us about love—and it probably is the case that millions of people who believe we do "fall" in love in an instant actually do so, or at least experience agonizing or ecstatic fits of passion. People tend to act the way they think they are supposed to, so if you believe you will fall in love "instantly" and it will be overpowering and irresistible, chances are you will and it will. But in addition to educating us in the ways of love, popular songs teach us about life. Take, for example, a song made famous by Tommy Edwards—"It's All in the Game." (I am picking old songs but ones which are good examples and help me with my task of explaining the social significance of popular music.)

This song is a statement about love. Love, it says, is a game, and, by extension, so is life. This game is not always happy and cannot be always happy. We recognize that tears *have to* fall in this game, so we are "realists" and not romantic idiots or sentimental fools. But though tears have to fall, it is all part of life and love and the game, and you can win the game if you have enough heart and your love is strong enough. Your heart can rise above arguments and that kind of thing. There will be setbacks, also . . . when he won't call. But you need not worry, for somehow, mysteriously he'll soon be at your side with flowers. Once there, he will kiss your lips (what else?) and caress your waiting fingertips, sending you into ecstatic flights of transcendent love.

In this song, which sees love as a game, as we might expect there is a strong element of fatalism—the same fatalism we find in "Some Enchanted Evening," in which we can rest assured that we *will* see a

stranger in some crowded room. Since the fates declare that true love will and must win the day, we need not worry about the setbacks we are to face, and *we need not do anything*, actually, since our heart can rise above any problem. Why this game of love is so wonderful even when there is so much trouble is not explained, but, as everybody knows, "the course of true love does not run smoothly."

The rather simple, 32-bar, and silly (despite its overwhelming seriousness) popular ballad with its verse/chorus and cloying rhyme scheme no longer dominates popular music the way it used to. It has given way, in large part, to rock music, which is generally electronic, often harmonically and linguistically complex, and usually overpoweringly loud. The visceral impact of rock, its ability to overwhelm you by its sheer volume, and to hypnotize you by its beat, suggests now that many people want something else from their music—some kind of shattering sensory experience rather than a lesson about love and life.

There have been a number of books written about rock and other kinds of popular music, and there is now a journal, *The Journal of Society and Popular Music*—published by Bowling Green University—devoted to the subject. The University of Illinois Press has a series on Music in American Life, there is the magazine *Rolling Stone*, and a number of other publications devoted to music. The popular music industry is enormous, with some thousand record companies, close to ten thousand singers, and sales of about a billion dollars per year. (The Beatles alone have sold five hundred million dollars' worth of records.)

There is some reason to believe that rock has "peaked" and is losing its popularity, but even if it does fade, its impact on the popular ballad and other forms of popular music will have been great. There is a world of difference between "All in the Game" and "Bridge Over Troubled Waters" or "Some Enchanted Evening" and "Suzanne."

## WHO ARE YOUR HEROES?

Every society indoctrinates its young people with certain notions about how life should be lived, what is important and unimportant, and how to relate to the society in general and various kinds of people (parents, teachers, women, leaders) in particular. One way societies go about doing this is by creating culture heroes, figures who are "larger than life" and who represent (or personify) the basic ideals and values of the culture. These culture heroes are created in various ways. In pre-literate cultures they are legendary figures whose exploits are passed down by word of mouth over enormous periods of time. In technological societies, which have mass media, they are often created by writers and artists who work in a number of different art and popular art forms, such as the novel, popular fiction, comics and the movies.

Frequently the heroes created in one medium are extremely popular in another, and currently all kinds of culture heroes are to be found in various media, sometimes in a number of different ones at the same time. Batman started as a comic book character, but was popular on television for a few years and was the hero of a movie. The same kind of thing can be said for various kinds of culture heroes, who may be successful in books, movies, and television—perhaps all at the same time.

Historically, the most important American culture hero is the cowboy. He is an extremely complex figure who represents a number of American ideals—innocence, nature, individualism, bravery and self-control, among other things. There are certain conventions for the classic cowboy story. It must take place near or on the frontier, in a specific period in the American past when lawlessness was declining but law and order had not yet arrived.

At times the cowboy story is the story of self-reliant individualism conquering the forces of evil—through the use of violence—and rewarded by pure love, but this is only one of many possible variations. Frequently the cowboy renounces love and society, and rides off into the sunset. In the film *Shane*, for example, we find an excellent example of the basic myth of the cowboy.

Shane, a stranger with "no past" (that he admits to) suddenly appears on the scene and confronts evil-personified in the form of a hired killer symbolically dressed in black. Shane destroys the killer and the evil forces that had controlled the town. He is thrust into a gunfight—a situation that he had wished to avoid—reacts heroically, and manages to preserve his innocence even though he kills. At the end he nobly forsakes love and rides away. The picture ends with the plaintive cries of a little boy who loves him echoing through the hills.

It is hard to explain why westerns are so popular. They are usually full of violence and aggression, which we vicariously "participate" in. They may serve, then, as a means of our ridding ourselves of (or easing) pent-up emotions and frustrations. Also, it may be that in an urbanized society, full of people who are crammed together, we derive a certain amount of pleasure in the spaciousness and scenic grandeur of the mythical west. And the capacity of the cowboy to *act* and the rather simplistic moral nature of the westerns, with "good guys" and "bad guys," reduce the burden on our psyches caused by the violence. In contemporary society we have rather ambiguous feelings about violence, and cannot get the emotional gratifications from it that we obtain in situations where violence is acceptable, or even necessary.

Despite the popularity of the cowboy, he is not, I think, the representative American hero. The cowboy is a victim of the past—which possibly explains his endurance. We can mythologize and glorify the past, read into it whatever we wish, so it doesn't become contaminated with the light of reality and truth. It is a dream world where we make things take the shape we wish them to, and we don't have to worry about the "reality principle."

But the cowboy had to "die" (as a legitimate culture hero, that is) when civilization caught up with him. When life became urbanized and institutionalized, there was no more frontier where "justice" had to be meted out violently.

The great American culture hero now is the detective: he is modern, a creature of the cities; he is representative—a "private eye" in a country devoted to private enterprise. And he is not crushed by the city, by the stupidity of society or governmental bureaucracy (especially its police officers) or the villainy of evil people or by fate. The detective is the great individualist who demonstrates that there is still a chance for the strong and courageous, that Horatio Alger's ideas are still valid, though now one must resort to more than just hard work and enterprise.

The detective is the rugged individualist who survives in an environment hostile to individualism; modern society demands conformism, servility, and its basic thrust is towards depersonalization and alienation. Mickey Spillane's tough-guy detective hero Mike Hammer is probably the best example of the detective—at least of the American form of this hero. Spillane is one of the top-selling fiction writers —his books have average sales of five million copies, and he has sold more than forty million books all together.

Usually Mike Hammer is characterized as a violence-prone sadist, and the violence and low-keyed eroticism of Spillane's books are given as the reason for their popularity. However, as John G. Cawelti has pointed out in an important essay, "The Spillane Phenomenon," Spillane's novels are very similar, structurally speaking, to temperance novels, which were popular at the turn of the century. As Cawelti puts it:

> . . . Spillane has always instinctively recognized the connection between his narratives and the popular evangelical tradition and has been able to tap the great passion which many Americans have invested in that tradition by embodying its central themes of hostility toward the sinful city with its corrupt men of wealth, its degenerate foreigners, and its Scarlet Women. Of all the hard-boiled writers, Spillane's art is closest in its mythical simplicity to the folk tale and in its passionate hatred and denunciations to the popular revivalist sermon.

Mike Hammer emerges then, not as a sadist, but as a would-be savior, and his great popularity with the American public reflects a fear held by many—that the mythical innocent America found in the cowboy stories is doomed to destruction.

The cowboy and the detective emerge as the two central and most important American culture heroes. The cowboy still hangs on, though he is no longer a valid symbol of American society, and the detective, in various manifestations, continues to engage our interest. Around

these two figures revolves a constellation of other culture heroes, such as the jungle hero (Tarzan), the secret agent (*Mission Impossible*), and the space voyager (Spock).
To find out about a society or about ourselves we can ask the same question—who are your heroes?

# GETTING THE MESSAGE

Hot Language and Cool Lives
TV Ads and American Society
Ads and Addiction
Print
Newspapers and Tragedy

# HOT LANGUAGE AND COOL LIVES

One fish always delights me when I take my children to the aquarium. It is a slender rather trivial thing which has the ability to puff itself up into a big ball and scare off other fish which might wish to attack it. It is literally a big windbag, yet this defense mechanism works—well enough, at least, for other windbags to be born and survive. The whole business is quite absurd except that it does work, and what is more fantastic, it works with people as well as with fishes. A lot of people are leading rather lukewarm lives, if not cool (and not in the sense of "good" as some use the term) or tepid lives, yet they describe themselves and their actions in terms of what might be called "hot" language.

I can recall once overhearing two bored youths at a tennis court. "Let's split," said one of them, a phrase that fits the schizophrenic nature of the times. Somehow "splitting" from a place is much more exciting than "going someplace else" or "leaving."

Is it not possible that there is a direct correlation between a growing sense of powerlessness and futility in our lives and the jazzed up language we use? The more you feel yourself diminished the more you "build yourself up" by using hot language, showing that you are in some kind of an "in" group, and know what's going on. It is only natural to try to represent one's self in the best possible light, but if we study the way people do this we find that, at least as far as the language they use is concerned, this hot or inflated language is somewhat self-defeating.

As everything becomes inflated and *tremendous*, the word loses its power. What is normal becomes tremendous. What then do we say about something that really *is* tremendous? It seems that the more we use hot language to add color to our otherwise colorless lives, the less utility the hot language has; it becomes devalued, and we have to work harder for less, so to speak. What used to be large is now "giant king size," and we have reached the point of no return.

Perhaps there is some kind of a searching for the infinite at work. In a recent advertisement for a humane society various kinds of memberships were announced:

Annual—$5; Patron—$10; Life—$100; Perpetual—$250.

A lifetime is no longer enough. We must have a rate for those who would be immortal. On the other hand, we find ads for insecticides which claim that they "kill bugs *dead!*" Death must be made more final.

It may be that we can now think of killing without death—for as everything grows out of control and the fantastic becomes the commonplace (men on the moon on prime-time television), the old words, like the old lifestyle, become somehow inadequate. We need more and more emphasis—we must be told that when something is killed, it will be really dead.

Television commercials have bred in the average American a skepticism that must somehow be overcome. We find all about us claims that are obviously absurd: on menus, travel brochures, bookjackets, etc. The law of diminishing returns is at work. Since people now believe less and less, you have to promise more and more to come out even. In this sense advertising is self-defeating for it has created (more than anything else) this skepticism which it keeps attacking and reinforcing at the same time.

The use of this hot language is symptomatic of a certain malaise affecting people, which leads them to believe that life must, at all times, be exciting, vital, dazzling, full of "fabulous" experiences that make one into a "fantastic" person. This is nonsense, obviously. Everyone spends a great deal of his time doing routine, ordinary things—even "world historical figures" such as leaders of great nations or movie celebrities. Thus, the use of this language makes us *devalue* our lives, since we take a rather absurd conception of what is normal, measure our lives against this false norm, and find ourselves wanting. We all want to lead "Giant King Size" lives in an age when there are few giants or kings. Since we cannot, we then define ourselves as leading lives of quiet desperation, life as absurd and meaningless, and try to escape from all this by consumermania, drugs, or some other kind of narcotism.

A distinguished sociologist, Leo Lowenthal, has discussed a form of hot language, the use of "superlatives", in the following manner:

*This wholesale distribution of highest ratings defeats its own purpose.*
*Everything is presented as something unique, unheard of, outstanding.*

*Thus nothing is unique, unheard of, outstanding. Totality of the superlative means totality of the mediocre. It levels the presentation of human life to the presentation of merchandise.*

He wrote this in reference to the tendency of contemporary writers to use superlatives in biographies done for popular magazines. Lowenthal noticed that there was a change from early biographies which didn't use superlatives and dealt with heroes of production to recent biographies (around 1940) which used superlatives and were about heroes of consumption. The superlatives didn't, on first sight, seem very significant, until their real function was discovered. This was, Lowenthal suggested, to create "a reign of psychic terror, where the masses have to realize the pettiness and insignificance of their everyday life. The already weakened consciousness of being an individual is struck another heavy blow by the pseudo-individualizing forces of the superlative."

This was written in the forties, when we had "stars." How does the ordinary man feel in the seventies, in an era when being a "star" is no longer significant, since we now have "*super*stars." When the star is relegated to mediocrity, what do we say about the average citizen? The fact that we now use terms such as the "little guy" is significant; his stature and significance are diminishing greatly, and he is on the verge of becoming a "forgotten" American.

## BRAINWASHING THROUGH THE BOOB TUBE:
## TV ADS AND AMERICAN SOCIETY

In dealing with television commercials it must be noted that we are investigating a kind of "art form" or "commercial art form" which, almost everyone agrees, has great power. Television is a medium that makes use of our audial and visual senses, and as such has greater impact than media (such as print or radio) which appeal to only one sense. As Alberta Siegel put it in her article "Mass Media Violence: Effects on Children" (in *Stanford M.D.,* Spring 1969):

*Humans learn most efficiently through vision and audition. Although information is acquired from the other senses as well—touch, taste, smell—the human is best equipped to handle information from seeing and hearing, and except in early infancy most learning occurs through these senses.*

*The young child learns how people behave in his cultural group by watching them and by listening to them . . . Even before he can understand language, though, the infant attends intently to the actions and voices of the people around him, and appears to understand gestural communication and the emotional nuances of vocal communications.*

Dr. Siegel is concerned with television programs in general, not with advertisements—and I may add that her conclusion is that "to the extent the media glorify mugging, mayhem and murder, they teach violence." But she makes the point that television stations argue that advertisements sell products (which means they influence behavior) and, at the same time, disclaim that television affects social beliefs and actions.

Because commercials are a kind of art form, and because art forms of every sort are extremely difficult to analyze in a manner that "commands acceptance" of one's findings, it is necessary to be cautious in talking about them. Especially when it comes to dealing with the psycho-cultural significance of advertisements. Nevertheless, I do believe that certain conclusions can be reached and supported with a fair measure of confidence. Generally speaking, advertising agencies have been concerned with only one aspect of commercials—their sales impact or "effectiveness"—and have not been concerned with other considerations. A great deal of money has been spent in marketing research along these lines, but even here the agencies can never be sure that just because a high percentage of people remembered a commercial they subsequently were inspired to buy. As one advertising executive put it to me (he is the creative director of a moderately sized San Francisco agency), nobody really "knows" what they are doing —in the sense that they have any sense of certainty that one thing they will try will be better than something else. That is why advertising men are always talking about "running things up flagpoles to see if anyone salutes."

If we take the fact that television is the most powerful mass medium presently available and add to this the fact that television is watched something like five hours per day in the average American family, we can see that it is quite reasonable to assume that television has had and is having an important impact on the psychological development of its viewers and on society in general. The average American youth has seen an estimated 18,000 hours of television by the time he finishes high school (as contrasted with 11,000 hours he will spend in the classroom) and has been exposed to something like 300,000 commercials.

At this point I would like to make a distinction between *instruction*, which I define as formal education by teachers in generally structured situations, and *education*, as that which we learn from all of our experiences. We find, then, if we recall what Dr. Siegel said about children learning from watching and listening to people, that commercials are "teaching" us all a great deal about life—often teaching us things that the makers of the commercials are unaware of. Commercials often have *unintended* consequences (such as reinforcing attitudes, giving people negative self-images, etc.) as well as the hoped-for intentional consequences—getting someone to buy a product or use a service.

For example, commercials provide "models" (literally and figuratively) of experience, but the models are atypical. Problems vanish almost instantaneously, and girls who were lonely and desperate become madly sought after just by switching to a certain kind of mouthwash. Headaches vanish almost instantly for those who know which

product to reach for, and the same kind of simplification of experience
—and I'm not saying anything about falsification of experience, which
is also often the case—is beaten into our heads time and time again.
The girls themselves also tend to be atypical. They are often volup-
tuous, exuding a sexuality which becomes attached to the product in
some way, or else women are shown who are rather banal and sexless,
as we find in many soap ads. The dull housewives really suggest that
women lose their sex appeal when they get married, and perhaps their
rationality. Anyone who can get excited by a kind of soap *must* be
stupid! I imagine the men who make these commercials do not hold
a very high opinion of the average American housewife. In the quest
for memorable faces and sales impact, the commercial makers loose
upon the public various figures who distort reality considerably—either
in terms of their physical endowments or their bizarre qualities. The
man who is continually bombarded by sexy women selling this
or that may start taking second looks at his wife and making invidious
comparisons.
Television commercials are often called "mini-dramas," and with good
reason. They can be thought of as condensed versions of plays, in
which all the action is reduced to an essential thirty or sixty seconds.
We might even say they are modern equivalents of the ancient morality dramas, except that morality has been replaced by consumermania as a *summum bonum*. These mini-dramas use all the
techniques of the cinema and some techniques that are even more
advanced than we find in the cinema, owing to the fact that television
viewers have been conditioned along certain lines.
Television commercials do not need *establishing* shots, shots which
set the scene, but can start in the middle of their pitch, so to speak. In
addition, techniques of the cinema such as multi-imagery, close-ups,
lingering dissolves, zooms, bright colors, hand-held camera work, and
quick cutting (to mention only some of them) can be used to create
excitement and stimulate the viewer. *The use of dramatic images,*
*music, rhythm, rhyme, etc., all combine to bypass rationality and shape*
*behavior.* Commercials through their imagery often have a direct,
*visceral* impact—and provoke gut reactions, in the literal sense of
the phrase.

Pop Culture/85

We know that on a per-second basis, commercials are generally much more expensive than the programs in which they are shown. As a commentator said about them (Jon Carroll, "Datebook," *San Francisco Chronicle*, December 10, 1967):

*. . . TV commercials are very good. They may be the best thing on television. They are frequently more creative, more witty, better photographed, better planned and better executed than the programs. They are, in many ways, even better than most movies.*

There is actually an implicit conflict between the commercials and the programs. It is in the interest of advertisers to have mediocre programs so that the commercials have more impact on the viewers' minds. As I concluded in an essay on non-linear commercials (*ETC.*, Dec. 1969):

It seems quite evident that in television—and we could project this to the other media—the influence of advertising is destructive and corrosive. It degrades the media and the viewer. In television, for instance, the commercials are at war both with the regular programs, which they seek to dominate by virtue of their superiority, and with the viewers, whom they seek to dominate.

The best of all possible worlds for the advertiser, I would imagine, is to have a mediocre program which is very popular—thus insuring a large audience to be exposed to superior commercials.

The argument to this point is as follows:

FIRST, television is a powerful instrument of communication.

SECOND, the average American watches television a great deal of the time, which serves to intensify the impact of television on his psychological development, and collectively, on society as a whole.

THIRD, television commercials (and television itself) offer us a model of life which is distorted and possibly destructive of rationality. It simplifies experience, suggests that all problems can be solved if the right product is purchased, and tends to hold up the atypical as typical (by implication).

FOURTH, I have suggested that television commercials, which are more carefully and expensively created, often have a visceral impact upon people, which in many cases is disturbing, since advertising often tries to provoke anxiety and feelings of inadequacy.

The techniques advertising copywriters use are often suspect. One of the main techniques is *irritation,* which seems to be most effective in selling certain products. At no time is the question raised as to whether it is ethical or legitimate to irritate people so that they can be induced to purchase products. Another technique is repetition, which sometimes in itself is irritating. A constantly repeated irritating advertisement, in this context, becomes a kind of mild torture. It too is morally suspect, since it is not very far removed from brainwashing; I cannot help but wonder—do advertisers have the right to "condition" people along certain lines? They are using public property, the airwaves, for private gain, and their ads may have anti-social consequences.

Another technique often used is what I would call the *exploitation of sexuality.* Beautiful women are induced to exhibit their bodies often in sexually arousing ways, to sell this or that product. I believe there is something intrinsically debasing in this, which may be one reason models are paid very high salaries. It has to do with the notion that sexuality can and should be exploited commercially, which suggests that it is actually a kind of prostitution. Sexuality is shown as a marketable commodity; perhaps, by implication, everything is. Thus sexuality is often placed in a schmaltzy, ersatz-poetical, sentimental-romantic ambience, calculated to make one think he or she has had some kind of a profound experience.

In a *Newsweek* article on "Advertising's Creative Explosion," (August 18, 1969) the following case history of an advertisement was described:

*Meanwhile, other clients had been attracted by their (Spade and Archer Agency) zany approach to even the most sedate products. For Leasco Data Processing, a $2 million account, they worked up a television commercial that showed an attractive brunette climbing into bed with her unseen husband, who is complaining about his job.*

*"They're not using my full potential," he says. The husband is then revealed as a Leasco computer. Leasco liked it, but CBS didn't. The network insisted that twin beds be substituted. And the "wife" wasn't allowed even to touch the computer . . . In any event, the result was successful in the way that counted. "Leasco is getting so many leads*

*from that commercial that its salesmen haven't caught up with them yet."*

The commercial is meant to be somewhat funny—for there is something incongruous about a woman with a computer for a husband. But the point is, in the context of this discussion, that sexuality is exploited, to draw attention and to surprise.

On occasion *humor and wit* are used, often providing genuinely imaginative and perhaps even pleasurable (especially when contrasted with the irritable) advertisements. Often, however, advertisers are reluctant to run such commercials since they think that humor demeans their products. The most famous case along these lines in recent years is Alka-Seltzer. The Alka-Seltzer television ads won many prizes for creativity and imaginativeness, but the company changed advertising agencies and dropped the campaign only to return to humor later with its famous "I ate the whole thing" and "Try it; you'll like it" advertisements. But even humorous ads can be harmful. Alka-Seltzer is a drug and it may not be socially useful to have appealingly humorous drug advertisements.

When you consider the techniques used by advertisement makers in terms of the various arguments about advertising found above, it seems quite obvious that television commercials are of immense importance as socializing agents in American society, yet they have been only casually investigated from this point of view. I have been concerned, to this point, with the impact of commercials and the techniques used in making them.

There is another aspect of commercials which should be considered, namely the theory of motivation found in them. I touched on this subject when I said that commercials tend to create feelings of anxiety and inadequacy. I would like to expand on this topic and say something about the psychology of "man" found in commercials as reflected in the kinds of motivations appealed to by the commercials.

What view of society and man is found in commercials? One fundamental motivation seems to be relief from pain, from headaches and upset stomachs, and *anxiety*, caused by feelings of inadequacy in some regard. The vast number of advertisements for drugs and remedies suggests we live in a society which is inundated with pain, especially splitting headaches and upset stomachs. *If we are not a sick society, as the revolutionaries argue, we are a society of sick people* who have to gulp down billions of pain killers, pills to relieve upset stomachs, pills to put us to sleep or keep us awake, pills to relieve us of backaches, etc. All this seems quite minor and harmless, except that the ads collectively give a picture of widespread misery, and the behavior model in the ads—pain, pill and pleasure—may be stimulating drug addiction among children who have been socialized by such ads and who find themselves in a pill-crazy culture.

The matter of anxiety is also a complicated one. If the Anacin, Bufferin, Di-Gel, etc., ads suggest that pain is a dominant motif in everyday life, the deodorant ads, full of girls with moist armpits, suggest something else—namely that we stink.

We stink! That, in essence, is the message that comes at us time and time again, and there is now no part of the body that cannot be creamed or spritzed with something to mask our natural smells. On the most obvious level, ads for deodorants can be seen as attempts by advertisers to scare us into buying their products. It wasn't so long ago that "because of that" beautiful young damsels (who didn't know they had B.O., bad breath, and sweaty underarms) led lives of quiet desperation. Now advertisers are more direct. "You stink!" they tell us, and so we buy deodorants for any and every thing they can think of to deodorize.

Consider the names of the deodorants. Ban, for example, suggests a rather Puritanical, legalistic frame of mind. Smell is, in effect, to be "banished" from your armpits. Arrid, on the other hand, conveys an image of sterility and lifelessness, of something aseptic, deserted—by smell, not boys, we must assume. Other names are more prosaic: Right Guard, Secret, Perstop, Mum.

The genius behind the deodorant is that of conformism: not offending others. It is obvious that using deodorants represents the acceptance of a certain kind of image of oneself (cleancut and inoffensive) and one's society. It is no accident, then, that hippies, when they react against our society react against our "Mr. Clean Culture," and are conscientiously dirty. And it is noteworthy that one of the things that bothers middle class Americans most about hippies is that "they smell."

As frivolous as all this sounds, the subject is an important one. What kind of a sense of self do people have who are continually tormented about various natural aspects and processes of their bodies? Is it not possible that a continual bombardment of negative self-images has psychic consequences that are harmful?

The motivations which the makers of commercials believe will activate people are intimately tied up with the "image of man" found in the advertisements—in the visual imagery and in the dialogue, which I will discuss shortly. I mention this because sometimes it is difficult to separate the images from the motivations, as I am doing in a rather arbitrary manner now. When deodorant makers tell us that "we stink," we find two things—an image of man as a stinking animal, and a motivation in man which is activated—to stop stinking, to be one of the clean-smelling and therefore presumably "happy" folks.

Related to relief from pain and anxiety are such matters as jealousy, being outstanding ("first on your block"), conformism ("*Nobody* doesn't like Sara Lee"), showing you are a success and are rising in the world ("Move up to Mercury"), and snobbism ("for the selected few . . ."). One other notion (among the many that might be considered in advertising theory) is that happiness can be equated with consuming. Buying certain things is at times a way of obtaining relief from pain; but at other times it is shown as a positive source of pleasure, and as "creative." (There is a study by Emmanuel Demby on "The Creative Consumer.") In this scheme of things creativity is no longer associated with powers in a person to make or do things (with clay or words or paint) but is now defined as being able to purchase things made by others. Creativity is passive!

All these motivations and psychological principles present a view of man which is oversimplified. Pain, which seems ever-present everywhere, is easily taken care of, giving, I imagine, a mild form of pleasure, namely lack-of-pain. But pleasure can be intensified and made positive by consuming the right things, which will show discrimination, creativity, taste, what you will, and in some cases take care of personal problems as well. Through this world of television commercials wander glamorous lovelies selling cars or tires, or young nymphs selling soda pop or toothpaste, stupid housewives excited about how white their sheets are (and note that married women are often portrayed as sexless drones), rugged he-men or slinky females who smoke certain kinds of cigarettes (though cigarette ads are now off television, fortunately), all in an ambience of middle-class affluence. And what about the commercial which says very conclusively, "some families have it, and some families do not have it," comparing a young, lively and handsome family with a very ordinary looking family. It's a toothpaste ad.

Besides having a great effect on those who watch these commercials (and by implication on the society which is comprised of those who watch these commercials), they also reflect certain strains and difficulties in our society. Many of the images we find in commercials are interesting and revealing—and are susceptible to interpretation. I have already said something about deodorant advertisements which foster negative self-images and seem to be based on an underlying repugnance for the human body. The point is that this attitude toward the body and various body odors is not natural; it is learned and taught to us by people who wish to exploit us, one way or another. We are taught, to put it bluntly, to feel bad about our bodies and to gain relief from these anxieties by using various sprays and lotions. The situation becomes exacerbated by the fact that there is so much competition among the makers of these products. The public is bombarded by commercials, all of which reinforce the basic unconscious fear that is foisted on us—that our body, which produces so-called noxious odors, is somehow contemptible.

I make a distinction between the manifest or conscious message and the latent or unconscious message. The manifest message is the sales pitch; the latent message is the attitude towards the body that is fostered by the commercial. I would not suggest that advertisers do this maliciously or are even aware of the psychic impact of the commercials. The negative self-images and feeling of repugnance for one's body are the product of many different commercials, all of which, when added together into a total message, have this result.

Commercials also assign "roles" to people, some of which are most significant. In the Silva-Thins commercials, a rather expressionless, distant (hidden behind dark sunglasses) male treated beautiful women in an almost sadistic manner—pushing them out of cars, being "unresponsive," etc. This presentation of the male's role was obviously distorted, but, like so many things which seem trivial, it may have suggested to large numbers of males (particularly impressionable adolescents) how they should relate to women.

The role of women in many advertisements is quite interesting. In an article called "TV Commercials Women Hate Most," the following report was made of a talk by a woman advertising executive named Franchellie Cadwell (June 28, *Examiner* and *Chronicle*):

*Miss Cadwell, in a talk to a group of Washington advertising executives, said the rationale behind most of the "demeaning" commercials is that male-dominated ad agencies think the nation's 66 million housewives are "possessed of infantile fantasies and a cleanliness neurosis."*

*She said these commercials presume that women never leave the kitchen. They're in there day and night. Not cooking, mind you—oh, no, if you think cooking is what American women do in the kitchen you've got it all wrong.*

*They chase tornadoes. They engage in heated arguments with doves. They have floor washing contests. Men . . . fly in from outer space or rise from the sink—to consult with them on household chores.*

Miss Cadwell added that some commercials do allow the women to get out of the kitchen, but the gist of her argument—that women are presented only in certain roles and often in a rather demeaning manner —is the important point. Even when the glamour of women is emphasized, there is also something problematical, for in these instances women are exploited as "sex objects," which represents a kind of manipulation or man-handling that is not very healthy.

In recent years men have been subjected to the same kind of an assault as women by advertisers, who have opened up a whole new market in male cosmetics and have made men style conscious. Evelyne

Sullerot, a distinguished French commentator on mass culture, has explained this phenomenon ("The Male Narcissus, A Shocking Ad," in *Atlas*, reprinted in San Francisco Sunday *Examiner* and *Chronicle*, October 1, 1967). She discusses a controversial advertisement that appeared in a French newspaper showing a "handsome young man in the nude, the outlines of his buttocks softly lighted against an aesthetic background of shadows," and says:

*Why all this hullabaloo? Because the pretty silhouette of Mr. Protopapas quietly challenges the most sacred taboo there is: that a man is not a sexual object and his body may not be presented as something to be lusted after by men or women.*

*. . . Masculine narcissism is based on virility rather than beauty. By defining himself as a subject rather than as an object, a man is not the victim of the way he looks. But though solidly based, this eminently protective attitude is unable to put up a strong resistance to views held in certain areas, to certain situations and above all, to certain economic forces.*

*For decades advertising has been presenting women as a sex symbol in order to make her buy things she doesn't need. Now advertising is trying to push the male in the same direction so that he, too, will define himself sexually by his clothing and the things he buys. The result has been to open up a masculine market where free play can be given to the trade in both necessities and superfluities.*

That the advertisers have been successful in convincing men to change regularly the styles of their clothes and shoes, to purchase various cosmetics and similar items is demonstrated by statistics for sales in these products, which show that hundreds of millions of dollars are now being spent for them.

This phenomenon has been dealt with by sociologist Charles Winick in his book *The New People*. The title of his chapter "Costume and Custom: The Vanishing Difference" refers to his contention that American life is being desexualized, and this desexualization is revealed in such matters as men adopting more "feminine" clothes (and vice versa) and using cosmetics. As he points out, "the cosmetic and toilet goods field's most rapidly growing segment is the manufacture of perfumed products for men, which has increased 400 percent since 1950."

I think that I have given some indication of what we must look for when we investigate the social and psychological aspects of commercials. We have to look carefully at such matters as: ONE, their visceral impact, which is a function of the cinematic techniques they employ. TWO, the theory of "man" implicit in the commercials—their psychology and theory of motivation. THREE, the picture of society they project, especially as far as *roles* are concerned. FOUR, the images we find in them, and the dialogue that goes with these images. It is to this last consideration—the images and dialogue found in commercials—that I would like to turn now, with an analysis of some specific commercials that I find particularly interesting.

Advertisement number one
THE STRANGER FROM THE HOUSE (TRIBE) OF LEVI
One reason this advertisement attracted my attention is that I happen to know the copywriter who dreamed it up. He told me that he has absolute freedom and the company does not restrict him in any way, which is something rather unusual. Most advertising agencies work under rather stringent directions and have to satisfy their customers, who are often conservative and unimaginative. In addition to the restrictions imposed on agencies by the companies, at times networks also cause problems. The point is, then, that most copywriters work within rather tight boundaries. Such is not the case with Levi's. "The Stranger," which is the title of the mini-drama, involves a mysterious figure who suddenly appears in a town where people seem to be colorless, and leading lives of monochromatic desperation. The Stranger brings people Levi's, which add color to their lives (and style), and then wanders off in search of other towns to save. We sense, from the mystical and dramatic quality of the commercial, that there is something remarkable about this person. He has a sense of mission and there is something perhaps "divine" about him.

Certainly, his identity, that of a stranger, is quite suggestive. What this commercial represents is a fusion of two themes—*the lone-*

*some cowboy* (perhaps gunfighter) who "cleans up" a town being dominated by crooks, and *the Christ figure,* who possesses mysterious powers. Both figures actually have an evangelical quality; their mission is redemption of fallen man. The Stranger is bringing "good news," namely that Levi's are colorful, in stripes and patterns, and have interesting textures. Levi's are not just blue jeans. After he has magically transformed the people of the town he disappears as suddenly as he appeared. The voice of the announcer is unctuous, and properly so, for we have watched a dramatization of a parable. In modern terms it might be described as follows: "How the mysterious Christ-Cowboy stranger turned the drab townfolk onto jazzy threads." I might point out here that I think this commercial is, in terms of its mission, brilliant; it is fascinating, beautifully realized, and remarkable. It is a satirization of the cowboy and Christ tale, yet it has just enough dramatic integrity so as to be taken seriously, also.

It is a double joke on us—a "put on" telling us what to put on! But it is not, if you think about it, very reassuring. We are given a picture of the general public as being in a rather bad way. The citizens are listless, colorless, drab, dull, boring, and unexciting. It is only through the intervention of a supernatural (?) mysterious figure that they are able to snap out of their doldrums. And all it takes is a pair of pants! Being dependent upon mysterious strangers is not a happy state of affairs; read Twain's *Mysterious Stranger*.

It is a rather amusing, and perhaps mysterious, coincidence that the House of Levi has taken on the function of the Tribe of Levi—for they are the priests (both of them) concerned in various ways with men's salvation and redemption. I happened to see this commercial while I was watching *The Immortal,* the story of a man relentlessly pursued—for his blood—by forces which have every technological contrivance at their disposal. Between the two of them, the program and the commercial, we find dramatic presentation of a number of feelings plaguing modern man: pursuit by mysterious forces, powerlessness (especially when compared with mysterious strangers), boredom, anxiety, etc. Placing the commercial in *The Immortal* was perfectly logical, since they complement one another perfectly. The title of the commercial, "The Stranger," has other social and political implications. Strangers exist where there is no community, no bonds among people. Indeed, just the opposite is usually the case: self-interest and the quest for personal advantage make everyone an enemy or a potential one, since his interests may conflict with ours. "The Stranger" in this advertisement is a producer, figuratively and symbolically, and the people are consumers, and those seem to be the only relationships of any significance. Their relationship of advertising and "producer-consumer" roles has been explored by Stuart Hall and Paddy Whannel in *The Popular Arts* (p. 317):

*. . . Since the producer is autonomous, with the means of production at his disposal, making decisions about production as it affects the profitability of his business, and the consumer is assumed ·to be the private individual making personal choices about the consumption of goods, advertising must legitimize the market relationship and define society in terms of its commanding images. Implicit in advertising as a communication process, then, is the alienation of the sphere of work from the sphere of consumption. Advertising sees us as individual consumers making private decisions at the expense of others in the universal super-market, the great bazaar: it cannot see us as users of a common stock of produced goods and services which we both help to create and, in our turn, need. In these terms, advertising is an extension of the market system and can be legitimately described as the official art of a capitalist society.*

*A market which is organized by this kind of art has the advantage of leaving open a wide range of choices. But it has the disadvantage of highlighting the personal, as against the social, consumption of goods and services. It defines all needs in terms of personal consumption, though it is clear that many of the real and pressing social decisions in our society cannot be adequately taken in this way. . . . One of the charges against advertising is that, by investing only those choices which we make as private individuals with the glamour of art, it depresses in the public consciousness major areas of life where social decisions are urgent.*

In this respect, advertising reinforces and reflects certain fundamental

traits in our society, such as individualism and privatism* (the neglect of social concerns). Thus, the final irony—"The Stranger" has been amongst other strangers, who, in a sense, must always remain strangers unto one another.

In the commercial, the role of "The Stranger" is somewhat unclear—he brings clothes full of color and vitality to people who are dull and drab—but does he *sell* them the clothes? The mysticism and pseudo-religiosity of the ad evade this question. The merchandiser becomes God-like, a kind of divinity, but he is not preaching a social gospel by any means. In fact, it is implicitly an anti-social gospel.

It may seem that I am persecuting this poor "Stranger," and making some kind of a monster out of a saintly fellow trying to make people aware of Levis. I may be overemphasizing certain things in the interest of calling our attention to certain psychological themes and socio-political implications that stem from these themes—but this is necessary because we are exploring new territory, so to speak. *Images are resonant, and have vibrations (cultural meanings) of great amplitude.* These "vibrations" may not be obvious, but they are there. People may not be fully conscious of what is happening to them when they see a commercial such as "The Stranger," but I believe something is happening which may be affecting and speaking to their subconscious states, and, in turn, influencing their actions. As the eminent motivation researcher Ernest Dichter has written, in *The Strategy of Desire*: *Whatever your attitude towards modern psychology or psychoanalysis, it has been proved beyond any doubt that many of our daily decisions are governed by motivations over which we have no control and of which we are often quite unaware.*

Images trigger our actions; not rational appeals, but emotional ones. We must remember that the function of advertising is not to inform but to persuade and this is facilitated by emotional appeals, not rational ones.

Advertisement number two

THE MILLIONAIRE WHO LOVES MC DONALD'S HAMBURGERS

This advertisement is a remarkable one which utilizes a kind of re-

*In *The New Industrial State* J. K. Galbraith argues that advertising has replaced Puritanism as a means of motivating people to work. We work so we can consume, not to show our love of God.

## GUM

Americans are famous for chewing gum. This suggests to me that they do so to make up for having been deprived of oral satisfaction when infants, when they were exposed to their first and prototypic *Metrecal*—their formula. There is also an existential reason: chewing gum is absurd! You chew and chew, yet you eat nothing. The process is all and gum is all process. By chewing gum, therefore, the American is making up for lost time at his mother's breast and lives a sort of bovine philosophy. Every man a cow in America, where, because of the decline of breast feeding, every man had a cow for mother—at least as far as his milk was concerned.

Gum might also be a carryover from the results of the schedule system that was popular in America until recently, when demand feeding became popular. It has been suggested by some that a generation of starved Americans (during their infancy, that is) was created and these people have assuaged their subconscious fear of hunger by filling their freezers with enough food to fill a small army. Gum would be a carryover from the days when these people kept reminding themselves that they could eat at will yet, for obvious reasons, couldn't eat *all* the time. Thus gum allows you to chew all the time and eat none of the time; you have either the best or worst of both possible worlds, depending upon your inclinations.

verse snob-appeal for McDonald's hamburgers, a popular chain of fast-food stands with quick service, a limited and inexpensive menu. I have always been interested in McDonald's (and other fast food emporia) as a cultural phenomenon of considerable importance, and their millionaire hamburger eater is, in himself, a compelling cultural image with all kinds of implications.*

We see a uniformed servant in a Rolls Royce transporting a silver tray of impressive size. It is covered and we have no idea what is in it, or what product is being advertised. The limousine stops in front of a mansion, and the servant carries the tray through great columns and down long corridors. Finally, he enters a huge room in which sits a man in a luxurious dressing gown. Everything to this point is connected with luxury, wealth, elite tastes and that kind of thing. The servant is obviously as snobbish as his employer, who sits alone at a large and ornate table.

The servant brings the tray to the man, and takes off the cover to reveal McDonald's hamburgers, french fries, and a milk shake. The servant stands at attention. The millionaire's face lights up when he sees the hamburgers and other goodies from McDonald's. Then he looks sternly at the servant, who hesitates for a moment and then, embarrassed, gives the millionaire his change.

The point is, we are told, that you can get hamburgers, french fries, and a malt from McDonald's and also get change. And the millionaire knows this as well as his servant. The image of the millionaire showing delight when he sees the hamburgers has also been used in magazine advertisements. It is, in essence, humorous. There is something strange about a rich and powerful man being delighted by something as common and cheap as a lowly McDonald's hamburger. It is quite incongruous and we are shocked when we discover what was under the cover of that fancy tray.

There is a good deal of suspense generated by the first part of the commercial, which is silent. This heightens the humor. On the other hand, the image of the rich man indulging in the pleasures of the common man has a comforting aspect. Almost anyone can afford a

---

*For a somewhat frivolous analysis of McDonald's hamburgers and American culture see the first essay in my collection *The Evangelical Hamburger*.

McDonald's hamburger, so at least some of the good things in life *are* available to all. The incongruity of having a rich man eat a common man's food is implicitly a reaffirmation of our basic egalitarian and democratic nature, despite all the trappings of wealth and exclusiveness in the commercial. "Don't you see," it says, "the rich aren't that much different from the man on the street, except they have more money. *They* don't think they are better than you are, otherwise, why would they be eating McDonald's hamburgers?" Of course the millionaire is not eating his hamburger in a parking lot or on one of McDonald's tables, but that is not the important thing. What is significant is that he is showing that he is an ordinary guy, who likes a good hamburger!

None of the above is explicit, but for the commercial to work there must be a number of common beliefs and attitudes in the minds of most people about all the things I've been talking about. I would even speculate that the creators of the ad probably didn't consider all its social and political implications, as far as class relations are concerned. This is because millionaires eating McDonald's hamburgers (and that sort of thing) is so acceptable an idea in the popular mind, and is so much a part of us, that we don't even think twice about it. We tend to see ourselves as a classless middle class people, though this notion may be ending with the rise of radicalism in the universities and with the impact of radical ideas on American thought in general. *Our equal access to McDonald's, then, becomes the proof of the pudding of our great democratic society.*

The whole franchise industry, of which McDonald's is a most successful example, has been interpreted as "significantly" American. These franchises represent the last frontier, so to speak, in merchandising— the last chance for the little man to own a business of his own. Unfortunately, so many franchises have been established and the competition has been so great, that large numbers of them fail, leaving the people who bought them with little to show for their investments. But this is a matter tangential to our concerns, though, in a sense, the McDonald's commercial may be ironically relevant here. After all, it is the wish of many Americans to be rich. The peculiar nature of American society, with its alleged open mobility (supposedly uniquely American and often tied to "The American Dream") facilitates this, so that the common man, at least so the theory goes, opens his franchise and becomes a millionaire. Granted there is a great deal of hard work, but we all know that "where there is a will there is a way." Perhaps, to continue with this story, he becomes a millionaire and is able to seat himself at a fancy table in luxurious clothes and wait for the butler to bring him dinner. What does he get when he lifts the silver cover on the tray? A hamburger! Was it worth it? Has he been gypped? This little story carries the irony in the millionaire who loves McDonald's hamburgers to a fanciful and absurd conclusion, but though stated in an extreme way, it is a question that a large number of Americans are asking themselves.

So much for the analysis of a couple of "culturally interesting" commercials. There are many commercials which have little cultural baggage or resonance, and others which, like the two I've discussed, have a great deal that is significant in them. Anacin ads, for example, are generally irritating combinations of everyday and common events (truck drivers with headaches) and mystery stories ("with more of the ingredient that doctors recommend most"). Laura Schudder commercials for Taco Chips show a *homunculus*, in whose hands regular size chips look gigantic. Saab automobile ads talk about "well built Swedes," but they mean automobiles, not women. When we become "aware" of commercials—of what they can do to people and how they affect society in general—then we can stop being manipulated by them.

# ADS AND ADDICTION: TELEVISION COMMERCIALS, DRUGS AND SOCIETY

"Many people mistakenly overestimate the role of willpower and think that nothing can happen to their minds that they do not decide and intend. But we must learn carefully to discriminate between intentional and unintentional contents of the mind."
—Carl G. Jung, *Man and His Symbols.*

"In contemporary America, children must be trained to *insatiable* consumption of *impulsive* choice and *infinite variety*. These attributes, once instilled, are converted into cash by advertising directed at children. It works on the assumption that the claim that gets into the child's brain box first is most likely to stay there, and that since in contemporary America, children manage parents, the former's brain box is the antechamber to the brain box of the latter."
—Jules Henry, *Culture Against Man.*

"What would you do if you found yourself in possession of an effective science of behavior? Suppose you suddenly found it possible to control the behavior of men as you wished? . . . I take it as a fact . . . If man is free then a technology of behavior is impossible. But I'm asking you to consider the other case."
B. F. Skinner, *Walden Two.*

"But the most important effects of this powerful institution are not upon the economics of our distributive system; they are upon the values of our society. If the economic effect is to make the purchaser like what he buys, the social effect is, in a parallel but broader sense, to make the individual like what he gets— to enforce already existing attitudes, to diminish the range and variety of choices, and in terms of abundance, to exalt the materialistic virtues of consumption."
—David Potter, *People of Plenty.*

In the past few years, drugs have become a national problem. Drug addiction has spread to the middle classes, and the use of "hard" drugs such as heroin has grown greatly, so we believe. Statistics on marijuana use show that large numbers of people smoke it and there is a "great debate" as to whether it should be "legalized," so that it will not lead to a loss of respect of laws and increased social disorganization. Also, it is hoped that if marijuana is legalized, in some manner, criminal elements will be deprived of revenues made from it.

With all of this for background, an interesting question arises: Is there any kind of a relationship between television and drug use? Is the drug problem, which, in its present proportions, is of recent vintage, related in any way to the recent and phenomenal growth of television?

I would like to focus here upon one aspect of the general problem—television advertising and its influence on our society as far as addiction is concerned. If television programs inadvertently glamorize hard drugs from time to time, television advertisements "glamorize" soft drugs almost all the time.

The fact of the matter is that a remarkably large proportion of television ads are used to sell "drugs" of one sort or another: alcohol, nicotine, aspirin, cold remedies, stomach remedies *ad nauseam*. American culture, in general, is a drug culture—and many Americans are "junkies," even though they would be outraged if you were to tell them so. That is because they are legal drug junkies who pop "pep" pills, sleeping pills, headache pills, weight reducing pills, breast enlarging pills, and almost any other kind of pill that can be conceived of. Sociologists have pointed out that being an addict to a large degree is a matter of *self-definition* (in the same way that you have to learn that you are enjoying a "high" when you smoke marijuana).

The "message" of these various "harmless" drugs is, in essence, the same as the "reward" offered by hard drugs—escape or easy and quick solutions (via chemistry) to problems. Except that instead of reaching for an Anacin or Alka-Seltzer you reach for the hypodermic needle, and "escape from the ordinary." I believe that the logical structure of these ads, which show pained, unhappy, troubled people in the "before" part and happy, satisfied, joyful people in the "after" part is an implicit inducement to the drug culture. It is just one step beyond from aspirin to heroin, so to speak; the principle is the same one: immediate relief and gratification, instant solutions to all problems.

Another interesting aspect of television commercials is the way some of them utilize broken continuity and multiple images to simulate a psychedelic experience and one which is not far removed from a drug experience.

What happens, I suggest, is that the need for drugs overwhelms our fear of the law, conscience, and any other force which might restrain us. That this is reinforced and facilitated by advertisements which offer a model of how to "Cope" and which tend to overwhelm or evade the ego is a hypothesis I make. I believe it explains the connection between the structure of advertisments and consumption—of goods in general as well as drugs in particular.

These considerations add up to the following picture. I have suggested, first, that America is a drug culture in general, though most people do not recognize it as such. Second, once the principle of taking drugs is established, it is not too difficult a jump from legal drugs to illegal ones. Third, the "model" offered by many of the advertisements for solving our problems is very much like the model implicit in the drug culture—a better life through chemistry. We believe in magic, so to speak. Say the right word (to your druggist) and take the right potion, and any problem or difficulty can be solved. For those who have lower "lows" and want higher "highs," aspirin is inadequate and the next step is quite logical. Fourth, the makeup of many advertisements is a kind of drug experience itself. There is distortion, images flash out at us in rapid succession and we have a *visceral* reaction which tends to confuse us, weaken the power of our reasoning processes and make us more susceptible to suggestion.

The amount of money spent on advertising drugs on television is enormous. (If you add newspaper and magazine advertising, you discover that we are continually bombarded by "Drugs and Remedies" advertising—enough to give us headaches and other problems which they claim they can cure.) In 1968, for example, "drugs and remedies" ads amounted to $76 million for spots and $182 million for national network ads on television.

These figures become more impressive when we see how large a proportion they are of total figures for television advertising. In 1964, the $206 million spent on spots and network advertising for "Drugs and Remedies" accounted for about a ninth of all television advertising, which totalled about $2.1 billion. But if you add smoking and liquors, you find the following:

DRUGS, TOBACCO, LIQUOR

Network ........................................ $ 297,000,000

| | |
|---|---|
| Spot ............................................. | 198,000,000 |
| Total ................................. | 495,000,000 |
| Total network advertising ....................... | 1,100,000,000 |
| Total spot advertising ........................... | 1,000,000,000 |
| Total ................................. | $2,100,000,000 |

What these figures show, then, *is that if you define drug advertisements broadly, to cover nicotine and alcohol, we spend about a half a billion dollars a year for these ads out of a total of $2.1 billion spent on all television advertising for 1964. Approximately one ad out of four, then, is a "drug" ad.*

If you accept the notion that we are at times motivated by matters which we are not conscious of and cannot control, the significance of all this advertising becomes apparent. We are becoming "conditioned" or perhaps even "programmed," though we are unaware of it all, which makes things even worse. Because we have the illusion of freedom, we are the more easily manipulated.

And if all of these ads with all the phenomena associated with them (as described above) occur at a time when there is widespread anxiety about our involvement in Vietnam, many great crises at home and a government which some feel is not doing enough to solve our social problems and restore the currently distressed social fabric, then government and law, in general, become devalued. Thus we find a society which takes drugs in prodigious quantities (but which tells some people not to) asking people not to drop out or seek to "escape" from life in society when the society itself does not seem able (or willing, perhaps) to solve its own problems.

The devaluation of law and the continued social chaos both nourish the drug culture. In a certain sense our drug addicts are casualties of our society, who have become desperate and have lost hope in politics and have retreated into themselves, trying, with drugs, to "fix" themselves as best they can. There is something ironic to the term *fix*; for the addict problems cannot be solved, so he tries to escape from them.

The noted semanticist, S. I. Hayakawa, wrote a perceptive article on television entitled "Who's Bringing Up Your Children?" which makes the following points:

1. "The child who watches television for four hours daily between the ages of three and eighteen spends something like 22,000 hours in passive contemplation of the screen—hours stolen from the time needed to learn to relate to siblings, playmates, parents, grandparents or strangers."

2. "All happiness, all significance, all values that human beings might strive for are translated by advertising into purchasable commodities."

3. "Even as they reject the culture as they understand it, through television, they miss the pleasant fantasies they enjoyed as children when they turned on the set. So they 'turn on' in other ways. Having scornfully rejected the notion that they can achieve instant beauty and radiance with Clairol, they espouse the alternative view that they can achieve instant spiritual insight and salvation with LSD. The kinship of the LSD and other drug experiences with television is glaringly obvious: both depend upon 'turning on' and passively waiting for something beautiful to happen."

What has happened, and it is understandable although quite regrettable, is that we have not seriously considered the psychological impact and social consequences of advertising, an industry that is now in the $20 billion class.

Many of the people who make the advertisements are probably unaware of the ultimate impact of what they are doing just as the people who watch these advertisements do not realize how they are being affected.

In one respect television and drugs are similar: *once you are hooked on them, it is difficult to get off them.* Withdrawal from drugs or of television creates panic, and figures show, for example, that the average household replaces or repairs a broken television set within three days.

Since television is so ubiquitous and all-pervading, it is giving American society a certain communality of experience. The very rich and the very poor, leading extremely different life styles, with different "life chances," perspectives, experiences, etc. share a good deal now thanks to television. If television functions as a kind of narcotic, this kind of addiction has spread widely.

All of this makes me wonder whether there aren't certain cultural drifts, some of which are related to television and television advertising, which might affect drug abuse. I offer here some conjectures which may have suggestive value, even though I cannot at this moment, prove them.

Is it not possible that getting "high" is a kind of moral equivalent to being a "success" and rising in the world? For those who cannot make it in the real world, and cannot buy all those things advertised on television, there is the innovation of drug use and getting "high" in another sense of the word.

And is not drug use a kind of ironic reversal of our whole consumer culture and conspicuous consumption? Drug taking (and I'm talking now about the really hard drugs) is just the opposite—*inconspicuous* consumption, though the same motivations are at work—a desire for high quality merchandise, "refined" taste, etc. Since the soft drug ads posit a world of dullness and pain, why bother? There is, in fact, a kind of parallelism between taking soft drugs as a kind of relief from ordinary life's pains and trauma and taking hard drugs as a relief from withdrawal symptoms.

For those who find life dull, getting involved in the drug culture gives life, so they believe, a kind of glamour—underworld associations, avoiding the police, a "community" of drug takers, pushers, informers, etc. The drug scene becomes the organizing factor in their lives in the same way that cannibalism was the organizing factor in the lives of many pre-literate tribes. There has also been a mythology about drugs built up. That most addicts lead desperate lives full of terror and despair is seldom or inadequately publicized. Most of the claims for "higher knowledge" under drugs have been shown to be spurious but every "out" group maintains that it has higher truths as a defense mechanism or rationalization.

The drug problem admits to no easy solutions. That would be, in a sense, a drug culture answer: if you have a problem take _____ and what is recommended is something that is equivalent to a drug, such as harsher *punishment* (i.e. bad-tasting medicine). I believe we have to redefine drug abuse as a medical problem and take it away from the police, who have a vested interest now in drugs. I also believe that it is useless to multiply anti-drug messages as long as the society behind the messages subverts everything.

I would, however, like to see something done about all the "drug" commercials I've been discussing: it would be best if they were prohibited or, if that is not possible, drug companies were prevented from airing the kind of ads they do. What has happened is that advertising has changed from being a medium of information, announcing the existence of various products, to a medium of education and persuasion, though it works in very subtle and often pernicious ways.

If we wish to do something about the drug problem, we have to be willing to make some rather fundamental changes in society. There may be a certain amount of economic dislocation in the television industry from prohibiting drug advertisements but television stations make great profits, so I understand, and also they would be the first to admit, I imagine, that the public welfare is more important than revenue loss from these advertisements. There is too much advertising in general on television, and getting rid of a number of annoying and socially harmful ads would be a good thing for our peace of mind.

At the very least, we should certainly have some alternatives to the commercial stations, and we need a greater sense of social responsibility on the part of the stations themselves. Perhaps we also need a better regulatory system, which has real power to prevent misleading advertising from being aired and to consider the social and psychological consequences of ads.

Once we realize that drug abuse is a social problem and not just a matter of this young person or that adult who happened to get hooked, we can do something—for social problems are solved by social action. We can develop institutions to help prevent the problems from developing, we can develop strategies to attack the problem, we can use our ingenuity and imagination. It seems to me that we will have to make some big changes and take some drastic remedies; you do not get rid of cancer by taking aspirins, and you do not get rid of the drug problem by putting out a few scare commercials.

I believe that we can solve the drug problem and will, for we cannot tolerate, for much longer, the destruction of individual lives and the social chaos caused by the flourishing of this pernicious sickness. We need to have some money for research into the relationship that exists between advertising and drugs, and advertising and other aspects of our society. We also need new channels of communication that do not have commercials and we need to do some social engineering in our society in a number of different ways, so that people will not lose hope in themselves and society in general, and take the mainline to lotus land.

# THE STOCK MARKET PAGE, CLASSIFIED ADVERTISEMENTS AND THE GOOD LIFE

Some years ago, *This Week,* a Sunday supplement with a circulation of many millions, used to advertise itself with the slogan "the written word lives." *This Week*, like many other magazines, has been a casualty of television, but despite the power of television to lure advertising dollars away from magazines and newspapers, print is still a very important influence in our lives.

This discussion will deal with print from a number of points of view. It will analyze the "formal" significance of print—that is, the print itself as contrasted with what the print says and means, which it will also treat. These two matters, the "form" and the "content," are related, since in many cases the form itself has a "meaning" and affects the content in various ways. Also, we will say something about certain interesting psychological, sociological, and cultural aspects of print.

Though magazines may come and go (writing of Michaelangelo or Marilyn Monroe), and books achieve best-seller status, followed by obscurity, and though we throw newspapers out as soon as we are finished with them, *print lasts*. It is tangible—ink on paper, and it lasts for a long time, especially if the ink and paper are of high quality.

Not only does it last, it is "real," it can be seen, it can be returned to . . . , it has much more "substance" than speech, which passes quickly into oblivion, unless we find a way to capture it on tape or some other electronic medium. This tangibility is important in some respects. We all want to have classified ads or stock market reports "staying put," so so we can look at them at our leisure, or return to them if we have reason.

The *linearity* of print, the fact that letters are made of marks, words of letters, sentences of words, and so forth is leading, so Marshall McLuhan argues, to the death of the print world and the development of one in which we are bombarded from all sides, an electronic one in which the media "massage" us, so to speak. (Although McLuhan suggests that our linear "book" culture is fading, he still relies on books as the primary way of getting his ideas disseminated.)

This matter of linearity is extremely complicated, for printing is tied up with the industrial revolution, in that the printing process is a model for that of the assembly-line, which functions much the same

way as print. By putting bits and pieces together you get a typewriter or an automobile or a pencil sharpener.

If time is that which sets boundaries for audial media (you can only get so much on a 33⅓ rpm record, or three-inch tape), *space* is the boundary setter for print, and space is the basic item which can be manipulated in print. Type styles (faces) themselves have personality and are suggestive but these considerations are tied to space. The amount of white space left around print, which has an impact on us and helps determine whether we see the print as "dark" or "light," is the controlling factor.

There are also certain historical associations tied up with print—we use "Old English" for formal occasions, script faces for occasions where "delicacy" is considered important, and so forth. The names of some of the faces are quite suggestive. We have "elite" faces, "bold" faces, "minion" and "bourgeois" faces, text faces, and display faces. With the development of reproductive techniques, there is now a strong pictorial component which adds another aesthetic dimension to that of the type itself, especially since color can now be controlled. But the pictorial aspects of print are somewhat removed from our considerations. Our discussion of the formal aspects of print has dealt with print's *tangibility, linearity, spatiality and certain psychological connections we make with specific type faces.*

The informational aspects of print are so vast and so much a part of us that it is impossible to deal with them except in a rather general way here. For the fact is that it is in print that man has recorded his history and told the world of his ideas, attitudes, feelings and even his "secrets." Learning to read—to decipher the remarks which made up letters and letters which make up words—is the key which opens up the world. Print is the basic medium through which man expresses himself and explains himself to the world and the world to himself.

One of the curious things about print is that often the most important aspects of life are dealt with in the most mundane formats. The classified ads section, in which we find advertisements for jobs, houses, and even lovers, are printed in small typeface and, from a visual point of view, are non-distinctive and insignificant. *The classified ads reflect, with compelling power, the anonymity and pettiness and alienation which is so much a part of our culture.* Alienation is a hard term to define satisfactorily, but it has something to do with feeling like a cipher and having little that is personal or individual about oneself. In this sense, the stock market page might be seen as one of the most graphic symbols of the alienation in our culture. There is meaning in the stock market page but everything has been reduced to symbols and formulae whose gyrations signal profits and losses to corporations (those vast and impersonal "artificial persons") and which ultimately affect the fortunes of millions of people who "play" the market, or who work for the corporations.

It is this monotonous list of symbols and numbers which is of consuming interest to millions and millions of Americans, and it is this page which reflects, with painful accuracy, the alienation in which they are trapped—ciphers reading ciphers which will tell them whether or not their bank accounts—ciphers—will be larger or smaller. What is grotesque about this in the American context is that this is a society which emphasizes self-determination and willpower, yet the stock market represents the direct antithesis of all this. It is impersonal, it functions in essentially random and mysterious ways, the individual has no power to affect it (except for certain big manipulators), and yet it and "free-enterprise capitalism," for which it is the symbol, are held to be the cornerstone of democracy. To the extent that Marx is correct about the mode of production determining the shape of a society, the stock market page might be looked upon as an art form which represents most comprehensively our culture, *reductio ad absurdum.*

If the stock market page, which shows how everything is interrelated but is impersonal, is the symbol of our society from the most general point of view, the classified advertisements or "want ads" represent our society at its most mundane and petty level. The world is reduced to 50 or 60 categories, starting usually with "Lost" and ending with "New Cars For Sale." Most of the papers have some kind of index, but this shows the total content of the want-ad section and not the way it is organized. In the *San Francisco Chronicle*, for example, the general categories are: Announcements, Automotive, Boats and Airplanes, Business Offers, Educational, Employment, Financial, Merchandise, Pets, Real Estate, Rentals and Sports. Under each of the categories are listed the various sub-classes. But the first ads in the want-ad "supermarket" (as they call their classified advertisement section) are for things lost and found, and this must be meaningful. It is in the want ads that the "little man" speaks—telling the world of an old refrigerator for sale, or of "proven" blackjack systems or of lost calico cats. There is a world-picture to be found in the classified ads, even though there is usually nothing but small type, some words all in capitals, and an occasional bit of art work (though for certain jobs in "Help Wanted" or car ads there is often a good deal of display, some art work, and much white space). The pages in the classified ad sections are "gray"—messages reduced to the fewest possible words, utilizing certain abbreviations and stacked one atop the other. Does the monotonous and tedious compilation of these little advertisements reflect anything on the part of the people who placed the ads or who read them? Does the "art form" reflect anything about the personality of the artist? And what of the content of these messages? We find in the classified ads a world of errors, of useless (or no longer desired) objects, puffery announcements (of "sales" and gambling systems), and an almost staggering clutter of services, notices, and statements. It is a study in chaos—a chaos in the midst of which, by virtue of its general categories, there is a semblance of order. But it is the chaos of the petty, the "silent majority," the "little man" who reads little boxes or writes little advertisements. The fact is that the want ad is just about the only sure access the ordinary person has to "publication," except for the credit card.

Print represents regularity in a universe of flux and change, if not chaos, and we often describe and help create the sense of chaos with print. In this respect the electronic media have an advantage in that they can actually create chaos and make it be felt, viscerally, but this effect is only momentary, while print's evocation of chaos is lasting. Thus we find a medium based on order and regularity reflecting the chaos and variety of the world and one which deals with our most important considerations (love, work, housing) in the most banal of formats. Television has become the dominant medium of the day but it can never completely replace print, whose "imprint" on our lives remains—for reasons explained above—fundamental.

## SHRINERS

The fancy titles Shriners give their officials are reflections of the basic American egalitarianism. We have no counts, dukes, kings and queens, and so, in order to have a bit of color we create imperial potentates, grand masters and the like in our voluntary organizations. The leader of the Shriners is called nothing less than "Imperial Potentate of the Ancient Arabic Order of the Nobles of the Mystic Shrine." This is, at once, a mark of distinction and a parody on the titles of royalty. The elaborateness of the title makes it possible to have a title, for in an egalitarian republican society one must not, at all costs, take one's self too seriously or have what are commonly called "pretensions."

As a counter to our Puritan heritage of simplicity, the Shriners wear fantastic oriental costumes. Since we cannot dress flamboyantly in ordinary life (without being considered an "oddball"), we seize upon the occasion of fraternal association to parade around in fantastic get-ups and thus take care of our need for role playing. The mystic hokum is a relief from the drabness of ascetic Protestantism, which has little to offer in the way of mystery and ritual. These associations, and especially the Shriners, give a man a great deal, then. He attains a certain kind of "identity," even if it is a group one; he can have "fun," and salve his conscience since he has done "good works," and he can wear exotic clothes and have fancy titles and "get away with it."

# NEWSPAPERS AND TRAGEDY

Students of the press agree that radical changes are necessary in the style in which American newspapers are written. Studies show that the average reader samples a paragraph or two of some of the headline stories, but seldom probes deeper. He spends most of his time on the sports section, comics and other entertainment features. Yet, newspapers structured on "light news" as it is called, instead of "enlightening news," are finding it hard to compete with other entertainment media, especially television. No other medium has yet to challenge seriously television's genius for being light-hearted and light-headed. *The New York Mirror*, with almost a million readers, folded because it couldn't compete as an entertainment medium.* Still, for the moment, most of the American press has yet to meet the challenge of finding a role that electronic journalism cannot play. The role will be something along the line of what is called "interpretive reporting," or depth analyses of the news, written by experts, full of "opinion," and ending up, I imagine, something like *Le Monde,* the distinguished French newspaper.

But all this is for the future. For the moment the newspaper press is operating more or less as it has for the last generation or so. The news services are the great beasts of burden upon which most American newspapers depend, which means that to a surprising degree our papers are "national." This is true, despite the fact that many papers are overloaded with local news, which seems to be the stuff of which profits are made.* (While some big metropolitan papers are struggling, many smaller suburban dailies are extremely profitable.)

There are, of course, editorials and commentators, but only some 10 percent of the public reads this material, so that the very features that make for uniqueness and differentiation in newspapers tend to be insignificant. Except for the particular choice of columnists, the pa-

---

*The folding of *Colliers* and *Look* and the precarious health of *Life* magazine suggest that only publications dealing with specific subjects and appealing to certain subgroups can survive now. Special interest magazines are flourishing while general interest magazines are dying out, because they can't compete with newspapers or television.

*According to statistics, some newspapers in certain states will not acknowledge that anything of significance ever goes on outside their borders. National and international news is minimal.

per's political position, and any peculiarities of make-up, the average American paper is a product of one particular technology, newspaper manufacturing, and really just one more product among many. To the extent that America is non-ideological, journalists are robbed of any opportunity to have separate identities, and to the extent that our two-party system dominates American politics, journalists are forced into a choice *between* and not a choice *among.* We are always forced to oversimplify, since our political tradition which says that there are always two sides to any issue implies that there are *only* two sides. It is no accident that Americans have been so intoxicated with the conspiracy theory of history. Over a century ago de Tocqueville noted that he knew of "no country in which there is so little independence of mind and real freedom of discussion as in America."

This would indicate that our press is a reflection, and a good one, of the pressure that public opinion puts and has always put on people to conform. Once "the people" makes up its collective mind, dissent is seen as something anti-American, anti-patriotic, and dangerous. Dissenters are ridiculed as "kooks," and harassed. In such an atmosphere it is unreasonable to expect to have a press of ideas and opinion. I might add that, to the extent that the press services are national, they tend to crush regional differences and neglect local issues except for scandals and human "interest" stories, which are entertainment features.

The latest trend minimizes what little opportunity there is for dispute in the newspaper press, for in the last couple of decades one-newspaper cities and chains of papers have developed. It would not be inconceivable, then, to find a city with one newspaper which takes one press service. This situation would not be ideal for "independence of mind and real freedom of discussion." Even if the newspaper press does move in the direction of interpretation, the opinion will be quite partisan. Europe has a "press of opinion," as it is called, but there are numerous opinions available in every city. This would not be the case in America where a one-paper city would be at the mercy of the views of the owner of that paper.

In addition to problems of conformity, the economics of the one-newspaper city and the press services, there is one other problem the papers face: staffing. The traditional training now for journalists involves a university education, usually with a concentration on writing and journalistic techniques. *Le Monde*, on the other hand, has experts in their respective fields writing, rather than experts in "writing." Consequently, *Le Monde* (and *Le Figaro*, which has Raymond Aron, for instance) and other continental newspapers are able to provide opinion of consequence. What this means is that professional and what in America would be insultingly called "academic" writing is functioning at the level of the popular press, though *Le Monde* isn't "popular," as we would use the term.

We find ourselves in a bind, I think, for we need various opinions but we can only get them, except for certain commentators like Reston, Lippmann, and Max Lerner, from people whose opinions generally aren't worth serious consideration.

Perhaps this is not too significant in that the real function of the newspaper, as I see it, is as a modern substitute for Greek tragedy. The Greeks had Euripides; we have the Associated Press, which, if it lacks his genius for dramatic profundity, eclipses him in terms of its breadth and eclecticism. The newspapers are full of tragedies: personal ones, such as deaths and accidents, and public ones, such as wars, riots, famines, and the like. They constantly remind us, through both repetition and detailed description, of the tragic dimensions of life. It is this aspect of the press that is all-important, in America as well as in foreign countries. Perhaps, to push this thesis a bit more, the essential difference between the American and the continental press is that the American press tells us, again and again, that life *is* tragic and the continental press tells us *why* it is tragic.

In both cases, and this is like Greek tragedy, tragedy is an entertainment, and a means towards a catharsis, except that now the entertainment and our tragic awareness become fused with life. Life becomes a colossal soap opera and as everything becomes tied to tragedy, tragedy itself loses its meaning and significance.

From Wire Dispatches

**ther**

Today's High Low 70s
Overnight Low Mid 40s
Sunny, Warmer
Probability of Precipitation 10 Percent
Details on Page 43

CHICAGO — Democrat George McGovern said last night that as President he would "forget about saving face," "command an end to U.S. involvement in the Vietnam War and send his vice president to Hanoi to speed the return of American prisoners.

"—Immediately derly withdr can forces Laos and C all salvag tary equ assign is req proces within

### Around The World

Communist troops continue to hold 13 towns within 25 miles of Saigon. p. 2.

Five more deaths in Northern Ireland raise country's toll to 600. p. 16.

Returning to the original theme of his quest for the White House, McGovern said in a nationally televised address the difference between President Nixon's policy and his is fundamental:

"It is a choice, after a between saving face or sav lives. It is a choice between more years of war, or years of peace."

### Across The Nation

Sen. Wright Patman, D. Tex., calls anew for Watergate investigation, p. 3.

Study concludes most diet pills are ineffective for weight loss. p. 39.

**McGOVERN STRAT** regarded the speech a in his challenge to Mr.

It included the fa mula of ending the ing, military operat and withdrawing forces within 90 takes office.

### Here In Ohio

e tax repeal foes split and ach other. p. 14.
ard of Educa-
rd stu-

Taped in Wa and aired on other station campa

# COMMON OBJECTS AND EVERYDAY ACTIVITIES

TOYING WITH CHILDREN:
Cashing in on the Kiddies


When the subject of toys comes to mind (especially around Christmas), we find ourselves generally in an ambiguous frame of mind. On the one hand there are all the pleasant associations connected with toys—shrieks of joy from the children, "fun," a few moments of happiness. But there is also the matter of money, for toys cost a good deal nowadays, and, like everything else, are getting more and more expensive.

I used the phrase "come to mind" purposely, since we don't really think much about toys other than in rather sentimental terms or in terms of price tags. Toys seem to be a special category of things, which, because of their associations (and perhaps some special memories we have of old toys we had) are placed beyond the pale of reason or thought. Giving toys is a gesture of love, and we don't like to be coldly practical about such gestures. This is particularly the case because in many respects such gestures often have a less pleasant aspect —that of *buying* love as well as giving it.

We may refuse to admit the thought to our consciousness, but in some cases parents give toys out of a sense of *guilt*—for having neglected the children all year long. (This same motivation is behind "Mother's Day," on which we strive to atone for a year of neglect with a gift.) The cost of the gift becomes a measure of the sense of guilt we feel and the amount of love we wish to display.

In order to take care of our needs in assuaging guilt, a vast and highly competitive business has sprung up, using every technique it can command, to get inside the heads of children and sell them toys. Toys are a multi-*billion*-dollar industry, and as the toy manufacturers develop more sophisticated ways of selling their products (if such is possible) there is no reason it should not climb much higher. In America we spend more than five-hundred million dollars a year just for dolls. We spend half as much money for toys as the Federal government does on education, and though these toys "educate" us in certain ways, for the most part harmful, we devote little attention to them.

"Just toys," we think to ourselves as we grab the checkbook, "though they seem to cost quite a bit." At Christmas time, a couple with four children can spend a hundred dollars without even working at it, and probably would feel that they got away cheap. One reason we are willing to spend so much for toys is that, for those who are affluent, the high price of toys hurts, but not enough to cause much concern. Also, the genius of our culture involves consumption. We have been born to consume, so to speak, and our advertising industry, a twenty-billion-dollar colossus, and the culture itself keep reinforcing consumption. We learn, somehow, that buying is a way of solving problems and gaining all (or almost all) satisfactions. In the case of toys, for example, we can satisfy our need for training our children to be achievers by purchasing educational toys, most of which are overpriced and not really educational. Virtually all the educational toy companies have been absorbed by gigantic industries seeking to cash in on the kiddies. Educational toys reinforce the belief that something can be pleasurable and "good" for you, thus putting to rest whatever nagging doubts may have existed from our Puritan backgrounds, which intimated that if something was pleasant it probably wasn't good for you. Toymakers, and all those with products for children, know that the locus of power in the average family is with the children, and so appeal directly to them, going over their parents' heads, so to speak. Saturday morning on television is an orgy of violence and consumption, with the children constantly bombarded with "tell your mother and father that *you want* . . ." messages. Some of the programs are nothing but extended commercials, with heroes who are toy figures. The Federal Communications Commission eventually forces these programs off the air, but generally by the time this happens the damage has been done. But even the "acceptable" programs are too heavily larded with commercials.

That is one of the reasons the toy business is so pernicious. It is terrible to think that toys are now an "industry" and that the basic concern of this industry is making as much money as possible, with little regard for the children who play with the toys. In a sense, *the toy business plays with children*, using them as a kind of resource from which money can be extracted. It is the most degrading of indignities, this commercialization and dehumanization of joy. There are just a few big toy companies which dominate the toy *market*, and that is what it is—a market to be exploited in the same way any market is exploited. The toy industry reflects the same processes and forces that

are at work in all industries: massification tending toward monopolization, rationalization, mechanization, standardization, and as these elements grow, the human factor is diminished. After all, as the advertisers and sales managers keep telling us, "desire can be created."

To see the manner in which toys reflect the basic values of society it is instructive to look at two items—mechanical dolls and spider (sting-ray) bikes, both of which have rather ominous aspects that are not apparent. On the most immediate level the toy business moves with the country—from war toys to peace and ecology toys, but there are certain forces at work in the dolls and bikes which reflect deeper levels of meaning.

Case Study Number One:
### THE LIVING DOLLS

We often find that there is more than meets the eye in much of our everyday life. Some of the more ordinary aspects of our experience turn out to have dimensions and hidden meanings in them that are truly startling. For one example, take a look at the new "action" dolls—the ones that grow teeth, drink, say things and perform in other ways. These dolls are expensive—sometimes costing twenty dollars or more. This is necessary because the dolls are advertised on television and such advertising is quite costly.

The phrase "living doll" is usually applied to pretty girls, when we say something like, "She's a living doll!" But think for a moment. What have we said? We've described living, vital beauty in terms of artificial, dead and generally over-decorative prettiness. When we say that a girl is a living doll we are not conscious, I believe, of the *real* significance of what we've said, though the fear of falling in love with a mechanical doll is not an uncommon theme in the arts. (Such is the cruel fate of the hero in *The Tales of Hoffman*, who becomes enamoured of a "living doll" and discovers that she is a doll only when she falls apart.)

This matter of the "living doll" often takes on more menacing aspects in such manifestations as Frankenstein and the Golem. Whatever the case, the fact is that the new "living dolls" are, in essence, primitive

*robots*. They look pretty, in their saccharine way, but they represent the same dynamic as the robot, and to the degree that we are all worried about being dominated by machines, and in particular robots, there is a threatening aspect to them. What is particularly tragic about the "living doll" phenomenon, as far as the toys our little girls play with is concerned, is that the traditional function of the doll has been reversed. *Now the doll "plays" with the child, who is reduced to being an attendant, who slavishly serves, her robot.* It is the doll that has the "life" now, with an electronic heart operated by batteries.

For example, there is "Dancerina" ($15.99 without batteries), which is "a joy to watch as she gracefully toe dances, bows, pirouettes, even turns her head—stops—turns again." Or there is "Tippee Toes" ($14.99 without batteries), who "drives her plastic go cart . . . stands on her head . . . and turns somersaults." As the blurb for this doll goes, "Just push the button . . ." Then there is "Baby Sing-a-Song" ($9.99) which . . . or should I say who? . . . "knows the first line of 10 of your favorite songs and sings them in a cute, childish voice when you pull her ring."

I will not even bother with Barbie and her "friends," who talk, bend and pose in smashing outfits (for which you can spend almost $300 if you get everything), or the tooth-growing, hair-growing dolls or other "living dolls" which appear on the market with increasing regularity.

In addition to reversing matters, so that the dolls play with the children, these "living dolls" prevent children from using their imaginations or having satisfactory fantasy experience, which is one of the more beneficial aspects of play. For the fact is, these dolls are *morons* —maybe even worse. And their capacity to speak a few words (at the pull of the ubiquitous ring) effectively prevents children from fully utilizing and developing their imaginations.

These dolls represent the actualization of a fear that has plagued modern man for many years—the fear of being dominated by machines, becoming servants to them instead of their masters. The pattern is being set. Our children are learning to wait upon machines (for boys there are soldier dolls that shoot, etc.) and it is not too far-fetched to assume that more sophisticated machines, perhaps 20th-generation computers, will force us to serve them. Maybe, in a few years, when you see a "living doll," that's exactly what you'll be seeing! (Curiously enough, this is what we have to look forward to, according to some toy executives, who predict a forthcoming generation of robots for us to "play" with.)

Case Study Number Two:
### THE SPIDER BIKE: AN AMERICAN ORIGINAL

What are we to make of the new spider-bikes, those flamboyant, ill-proportioned grotesques which now dominate the American bicycle scene? The bicycle is a ubiquitous, and until recently, relatively uniform type of transportation. Most bikes are thin-wheeled, with light frames—similar to what we used to call "English style" in reference to a popular English brand, the Raleigh. In America, however, we developed the balloon tire bicycle in the thirties, an innovation on the English style, and this led, ultimately, to the spider bike, or "Sting Ray" as one manufacturer calls it. These bicycles are interesting because they are unique—American originals—and because they reflect, in mechanical form, many of the forces at work in American society, and many of its distorted aspects.

The bicycles are studies in self-deception: they are bikes which think they are motorcycles. Thus we find they have "high rise" handlebars, and items found on many motorcycles. Thanks to the rear tires (which come in various styles, depending upon what is to be done with the bicycle), it is possible to do one-wheel stands, a popular motorcycle trick.

These bicycles are relatively expensive, and can run into nearly a hundred dollars if you wish to indulge in all the flashy extras and deluxe features. You can get five-speed stick shifts,* souped-up banana seats called "glitter sitters," bright "glitter grips" for highrise handlebars, and chrome plated fenders, to mention a few of the "options." In addition, the manufacturers are beginning to introduce model changes, just as in the automobile industry. For example, Schwinn

---

*Sears advertises "five on the floor" stick gear shifts, which suggests the four on the floor gear shifts of sports cars.

introduced a new model called the "Ram's Horn," which is a light-weight, highrise five-speed Sting Ray, with handlebars that curve around like a ram's horn.

The development of the Sting Ray and its brethren only carries to a somewhat mad conclusion what was evident in the old balloon tire bike: a vehicle fashioned by American character and culture. The balloon bikes, called "trucks" in the trade, represented American ruggedness and masculinity. That it was stupidly inefficient did not matter. The thick tires and cumbersome frame forced the American child to pump strenuously and use a tremendous amount of energy, since the weight and friction were considerable. But it was worth it to have a rugged bike for future rugged individualists instead of those effeminate European thin bikes, with their narrow tires and gears. This balloon-tire bike represents a simplistic Americanization of the bicycle, but the genius of America was yet to manifest itself—it had to wait for the likes of the spider bike, the *ne plus ultra* of Americanism. As I see it, the spider bike reveals a great deal about contemporary American society. For one thing, it symbolizes the lost youth of the American child. Despite all the talk in America about how glorious childhood is, the various pressures in America all conspire to eliminate more and more of childhood, and make young people want to mature as quickly as they can. Thus we force young people together at very early ages and they stay together—going steady, and so on. We put young boys into long pants at a very early age, and once in long pants they learn, subtly, to act like grown-ups. Thus, young children imitate grown-ups by changing their bicycles into grotesques such as sting ray bikes, whose proportions are simply monstrous.

In addition, there is the matter of education for consumption. With the introduction of "style" into bikes, the young person learns to go through the motions as his father does when buying a car. There are options to consider, there is status to be gained, a lifestyle to be revealed. A few years of spider bikes and you are ready for the next step: buying automobiles, then anything and everything else. The spider bike, then, is grotesque. It symbolizes a perversion of values, a somewhat monstrous application of merchandising and salesmanship that I believe has got out of hand and led to grave distortions in American society. Young boys and girls ride about on bikes whose names suggest potency and death, bikes which make them think they are grown-ups and which teach them the fine art of consumption. The same anti-social forces, which are destructive of personality as well as community, can be found in other popular toys and games such as Monopoly (ruthless, cut-throat capitalism), Blitzkrieg (the Panzer mentality), and Hotwheels (vulgarity plus consumerism). If a society's spirit and values are reflected in its toys—and I think toys are one of the best indicators of such things—then we Americans have little reason for confidence for the future. Recently there has been a bit of protest about unsafe toys and unhealthy ones, but what few good toys there are—which children enjoy and which foster imagination and creativity—are lost in a tidal wave of expensive yet unsatisfying junk that comes flooding through the stores every year.

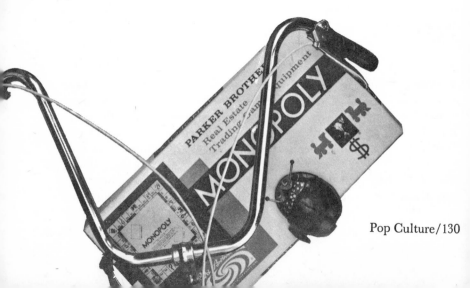

# THE GENDER OF THE BLENDER

In a feature story on Frank Sinatra, *Newsweek* mentioned that he had a $100,000 kitchen in his home. The fact that *Newsweek* saw fit to mention this, or that Sinatra found fit to indulge himself in this luxury, testifies to the importance of the kitchen in the American house. That is, I must add, to its psychological importance as the center of "goodness," the really *American* room in the house, the place (and the only place, except for the bathroom) where the American genius for mechanization, automation, control, efficiency, and cleanliness can really be manifested. The modern American kitchen is really a super-kitchen, full of devices to take the labor out of everything. Yet, does it produce any better food than an old fashioned kitchen? It it really, more livable (or even livable at all)?

What is most curious about the new American kitchen is that it tends, more and more, to move away from the "homey" place, full of sunlight and good smells, to the cafeteria or luncheonette ideal, with formica-topped tables, stools and counters, and the other paraphernalia of commercial restaurantry. The kitchen is, generally speaking, the woman's domain and yet it is increasingly less feminine and more like something we might expect to find in the inside of astronauts' rockets. The human touch has almost been taken out of cooking, and a curious situation now exists. As foods become more and more pre-cooked and quick-cooked, less time is necessary to prepare them. (The ultimate is a pre-cooked or frozen product which can be eaten, package and all. In the future, we may even expect, I imagine, a food product that comes in an edible package, that cooks itself, and that eats itself.) Why then, we may ask, are kitchens more and more elaborate?

There are a couple of answers to this question. For one thing, the kitchen represents the only place for the builder to show *his* genius, his imagination, in producing a labor-saving "modern" house. Also, a kitchen serves to demonstrate the status of the people who use it. (If Sinatra's kitchen cost $100,000, what could the house have cost?) A kitchen is one of the best places where a couple's "life conception" can be made visual, and the life conception of the ordinary middle class person is decidedly what might be called scientific-technical rather than humanistic.

As I see things, then, the elaborate kitchens we see advertised in the new homes are monuments to a conception of life (or, of eating) that no longer is valid. Everything is there for wholesome cooking in the "farm-wife" tradition; it should be made easier by electric mixers, big ovens, not to speak of electric can-openers, knives, etc. But what are the stoves used for: frozen apple pies, cakes, or quick-mix ones. There is a great deal of home cooking still going on, but the tremendous success of frozen foods and cake mixes testifies to the fact that many American housewives do not want to bother. Breadmaking is a lost art at home. Bread comes frozen now, for those who want to have home-made bread without the fuss.

A new image has forced itself into the American culinary imagination. Instead of a gray-haired, rosy-cheeked, smiling "mom" making apple pies, the "new mother" pops a frozen apple pie into the stove (from the freezer), opens cans and packages—and, Voila!—dinner. I have not mentioned the TV dinner, which is the ultimate in rationalized, modern eating. It is for  people who want to stay at home yet eat in an automat. The end of all this is to change eating from a pleasurable activity with psychological importance (the sense of community that comes from eating together)  into a physiological process pure and simple, *reductio ad ulcerum*. But there is another subject, related to this one, that I should like to mention.

If the modes of production and technology help determine our consciousness, as Marx says they do, we are led to a very interesting question: what is the significance of all the machines we have invented for the housewife? What do they tell us about American society? About women? About our way of life? I have previously discussed the American kitchen, in general, but now would like to focus attention on the various items that make up the modern, mechanized American household. In a very real sense the kitchen, the most important part of the home, is a reflection of the overwhelming impact of industrialism, machine technology, and automation on the American consciousness. We now have electric can-openers, electric knife sharpeners, electric knives, electric mixing machines, not to speak of such standard items as stoves, refrigerators and freezers.

But why so many appliances? American women spend most of the money in a household, so it is understandable that products appealing to them, designed to save them time and effort, have a better chance of being sold than other types of products. Still, I would suggest that there is another reason, namely, that these machines represent modern ways of satisfying basic instincts and psychic needs found, at this time, overwhelmingly in Americans. (It may be because we are wealthy enough to indulge ourselves that we use these particular ones.)

To see what I am talking about, look at the following chart which lists some of the more important appliances and what I think (or have guessed) are their basic functions in satisfying instincts and psychic needs:

APPLIANCES AND NEEDS

| Appliance | Instinct | Psychic Meaning |
|---|---|---|
| Freezer | Hoarding, pack-rat | Avoid hunger, conserve time |
| Washing machine | Cleanliness | Avoid death (which is close to dirt) |
| Electric knife | Treat from delicatessen | Good things are yours |
| Iron | Orderliness | Triumph over chaos (world can be made sensible) |
| Vacuum cleaner | Ingestion, incorporation | World can be made better (dirt eliminated) |
| Mixer | Make messes | Messes are part of things, become meaningful ultimately |
| Electric can-opener | Power over civilization, open Pandora's box | Free to be creative |

The basic function of a freezer is to satisfy the hoarding or "pack-rat" instinct. With a full freezer you know that you never need starve. The rationalization for getting a freezer that housewives use is that they want to save money and "have things on hand." Yet freezers cost at least a couple of hundred dollars to purchase, use electricity, and depreciate at such a rate that it is questionable how much money is saved by having one. And if anything goes wrong, the price of repairs being what it is, any arguments about economizing become untenable.

The main function of a freezer, then, is psychic or psychological: it reassures one. In addition, in line with the increasing institutionalization of private life, with the desire people seem to have to imitate commercial establishments, the freezer makes every apartment a little supermarket. Lastly, the freezer represents a victory over time, and ultimately death. With a freezer time stands still—at least for the things you put in it. They move out of time magically by virtue, somehow, of the magic of cold. An organization is working on the principle of freezing people just before they die, keeping them in that stage until medicine has advanced to the stage where it can fix their once-fatal ills, and then reviving them.)

There is something interesting to notice about the list of appliances above. With the exceptions of the electric knife (a man's gadget, really—since men usually do the carving) and the iron, all the other appliances are involved with what Erik Erickson calls the "incorporative mode," an essentially feminine mode that involves "taking in." All the devices are technological and mechanical extensions of the feminine mode. According to this, then, we find that the vacuum cleaner is the ultimate in the incorporative type of appliance. But we also find incorporation in varying forms of importance in the other appliances such as the refrigerator, the freezer, the washing machine and dishwasher, the blender, the mixer and the electric can-opener. The last three items may be considered second-level devices, in that the blender and mixer involve just a little bit of incorporation and the electric can-opener is a device for opening up already-incorporated entities.

I would say, then, that it is possible to classify household appliances and perhaps machines in general according to gender—just as electricians call plugs "male" and "female." There is at least, I must add, a certain poetic justice to what I consider to be a sad fact—the inundation of the American household by machinery. At least in the kitchen, the machines, which have been invented for women, are feminine ones.

These appliances also give women the opportunity to indulge in a woman's prerogative—changing her mind. It has been found that when many of these appliances are put on the market they are considered luxuries by women, but invariably, after a few years they change categories and are considered necessities. Could this be because the housewives, themselves, are taken in?

## E PLURIBUS UNUM

The food blender is a symbol of what is often called "cultural homogenization," and is much more sophisticated an artifact than our old-fashioned "melting pot," which scholars tell us never worked anyway. The blender, which functions on the same principle as a garbage disposal, can turn everything into a uniform slush. Foods lose their identity as the blender blades reduce them to a liquid. All differentiation is eliminated, all identity is pulverized into fluid that represents the "most common denominator" of everything that went in, yet is not like any of the ingredients.

The blender is a new fad in American cookery, feeding, in part, on the same cultural values that led to the development of pressure cookers: a passion for saving time and a love of power. Blenders are symbols of the end of America's vaunted cultural pluralism: divergent strains are mixed until they become blobs in which all the uniqueness and every interesting variation is broken down, leading to a smooth, bland paste.

# THE SECRET SIGNIFICANCE
# OF SOFT DRINKS

It is possible, I think most people would agree, to make certain generalizations about national preferences as far as beverages are concerned. Thus, the French, Italians and Spaniards (Mediterranean peoples) are wine drinkers and coffee drinkers; the English, Germans, Dutch, Scandinavians and Americans (Atlantic Peoples) are beer drinkers, and, except for the British, coffee drinkers. The Americans and the British are great hard liquor (fermented grains) drinkers, whereas the Europeans tend to be brandy and cognac (fermented wine) drinkers, though hard liquor is making its way all over the world.

Two of the most important types of American beverages, however, are the ubiquitous *Coca-Cola*, which has spawned a whole genre of soft-drinks everywhere, and the malted milk. The latest refinements in soft-drinks are diet soft-drinks, which permit one to have the best of both worlds*: pleasure (quench thirst?) without consequences (getting fat).

This catalogue, which is very general, is not meant to suggest that Americans don't drink a great deal of wine (they do) or tea (they are beginning to), but Americans are not wine drinkers or tea drinkers as a rule. The following chart presents the dynamics of drinking in a more understandable and obvious manner:

### NATIONAL BEVERAGES

| Country | Mild Alcoholic Beverages | Meal or Dessert Beverages | Miscellaneous Beverages | "Hard" Liquor |
|---|---|---|---|---|
| America | Beer | Coffee | Coca-Cola, Malted Milk | Whiskey |
| Great Britain | Beer | Tea | Derivative carbonated beverages | Whiskey |
| France | Wine | Coffee | Derivative carbonated beverages | Cognac, Brandy |
| Italy | Wine | Coffee | Derivative carbonated beverages | Cognac, Grappa |

We have not been particularly creative in terms of developing different kinds of alcoholic drinks, as the French or Italians have, for instance. They make drinks out of everything imaginable, from artichokes to flowers; where we have been inventive is in producing

*You can now have your "cake" and drink it, so to speak. The recent discovery that cyclamates may cause cancer was a complicating factor, but other sweetening agents have been found and the pleasure-without-pain principle is still operating.

mass-consumption, mass-production, soft–drinks of which *Coca-Cola* is the best known example. A cola is defined as a carbonated soft-drink flavored with extracts from coca leaves, kola nut, sugar, caramel, plus acid and aromatic substances. A *Coca-Cola* generically is a distant cousin to cocaine—the relationship is obvious just in the makeup of the words. Cocaine is a narcotic and local anesthetic, and both of these qualities, I would say, suggest something about American life. To the extent that *Coca-Colas* are second-rate narcotics and anesthetics, they represent an attempt, which is unconscious, by Americans to move beyond reality, to escape it. Thus "The Pause That Refreshes" can be understood in several ways: on the most literal level it cools us off, it freshens us up (and, remember, freshens means *arouse* and *stimulate*) ; also, on another level, it allows us to escape from everyday life by moving into some kind of a dream world or by dulling our senses so that the real world doesn't impinge on us so greatly. The appeals that *Coca-Cola* and *Pepsi-Cola* make stress youth, which points to the fact that these beverages are now being palmed off as elixirs—prolonging youth, changing base metals to gold (old age to adolescence) and renewing. Although both the colas present images of cleancut youth having "fun," it is well to remember that one of the meanings of refresh is to arouse. The cleancut, good-looking girls who drink the frosty colas are, at the same time, both escaping from the real world, its pains and inhibitions, and being aroused. In that sense, the colas are more involved than malted milkshakes, which represent a desire for the breast and the simplicity and serenity of infancy. It has been pointed out that the *Coca-Cola* bottle does look like a breast and quite possibly functions as a breast substitute for many people. Psychologists have suggested that people think of soft-drinks as luxury items with which they can reward themselves. The size of the industry and the spread of *Coca-Cola* throughout the world make it hard to offer generalizations about the significance of colas and American society, but there are several factors that must be considered. First, much *Coca-Cola* is consumed because it is one of the few safe things to drink in many countries. Secondly, it is very American, and for many people partaking of *Coca-Cola* involves being progressive, being

"American." So despite its world-wide popularity *Coca-Cola* and its competitors are essentially American phenomena and have meaning and relevance as far as the American scene is concerned. The latest phenomenon in the soft-drink industry involves "diet drinks," that is drinks with sugar-substitutes that cut down on the calories and yet provide all the "pleasure" that is desired. Diet drinks such as *Tab, Diet-Pepsi,* etc. work on the principle I call "The pleasure without consequences wish," and as such, are a triumph over some traditional American conceptions and are perhaps the hallmarks of a new society.

One of the great distortions in the American mind is that the Puritans were all sour and solemn. From them, according to popular belief (which is wrong) we discover that all pleasures have their consequences, that you cannot have pleasure without pain, and as it is thought, pain is a necessary part of life—perhaps even the most important part. According to this logic, whatever is pleasant is really bad for you and whatever is unpleasant (such as foul tasting medicine) is in reality good for you. Thus, the Puritans are supposed to have told us, you cannot have your pleasure without consequences, so if you drink *Coca-Colas* you will get fat. With diet drinks, all of a sudden you learn that you can have your *pleasure without consequences*! You can guzzle soft-drinks until you are bloated like a pig and not worry—since there are only five or six calories in every bottle of the diet drinks.

How this principle will affect the regular colas is hard to know. The two kinds of colas represent different principles: escapism versus pleasure, here and now, without consequences. I suspect that the major market for the diet drinks is calorie-conscious men and women, so that diet colas are not quite as significant as their parents, and despite their rocketing sales, are not so popular yet. When you join the *"Pepsi Generation,"* then, not only are you trying to escape your individual identity and merge into some kind of a group, but you are also trying to escape yourself and ultimately the world.

I might add, in closing, that *Coca-Cola's* rationale is a typically conservative American one, so that we have the fitting parallel of an American product mouthing an American "line." In a little brochure entitled "Why" that explains *Coke's* popularity we find that it is "pure as sunlight" (for the Puritan in us), natural—ingredients from nine countries but "no other flavoring agents are added" (for the a-historical American) and relatively low in calories (*Coke* has 12.1 calories per ounce versus 12.2 for imitators). But the main argument is a variation of Pope's "Whatever is, is right." *Coke* says that its popularity "must be deserved" and "it had to be good to get where it is." Its success becomes its justification. What we have then is a perversion of Pragmatism which says, more or less, that if something is good it will work, *not* if something works it is good. With *Coke's* type of argument there is no room for change and no justification for anything but "success." This emphasis on achievement, regardless of the means used, is an American characteristic which numerous sociologists have discussed in great detail.

*Coca-Cola* has just adopted a new advertising theme, "Things Go Better With Coke," which suggests that it is somehow instrumental in improving the world.** Despite the fact that billions of Cokes are consumed every week, things don't seem to be getting any better. That, perhaps, is the answer. If you have enough Coke, if you anesthetize yourself sufficiently, things seem to be better than they are.

---

**Since I wrote this, Coke switched its advertising theme to "It's The Real Thing," which is ironic, for as a second-rate narcotic, it most certainly isn't the "real" thing.

# CORN FLAKES AND WORLD DOMINATION

Since 1894, when Dr. John H. Kellogg created what was to become the corn flake, the ready-to-eat breakfast cereal industry has prospered mightily. It is estimated that more than 100 million Americans eat these breakfast cereals regularly, and the business has grown in the last twenty years from $180 million to nearly a billion dollars per year. There are now about 100 different kinds of cereals—from the standard corn flakes and shredded wheat to esoteric niceties such as *Cocoa Krispies, Smacks, Stax, Bran Buds, Cap'n Crunch, Sugar Pops,* and *Crunchy Granola.*

Several trends are seen in the cereal business: first, for the children's market there are pre-sweetened cereals with frosted flakes of one sort or another, and second, for the adult market, there are high-protein creations. One of these high-protein cereals, *Total,* claims to supply all the vitamin needs of the day. Eating breakfast cereal has become part of the American way of life and more or less taken for granted. The per capita consumption of these cereals has risen to 6.1 pounds per year, which is a great deal, since cereal is very light and rather expensive, often costing more than fifty cents for a medium-sized box. What I find most interesting about the cereal phenomenon is that a look at a family's cereals allows you to tell where the locus of power is in the family. The sugar-coated (and more expensive) cereals are often advertised on television, especially children's shows, and the children *demand* to have them. That is the American way: children are the equals of their parents and their wishes, especially in the all-important field of consumption, must be respected.

The industry itself is fiercely competitive and engages in high-powered industrial espionage to find out what rival companies are doing. Kellogg, with close to 45 percent of the business, dominates "the cereal battlefield," but there are five other large companies which compete with it: General Mills, Post, Quaker, National Biscuit Co. and Ralston Purina.* All of these companies must keep introducing new cereals, yet must be careful when they do so, since it costs about $10 million to market a new cereal.

---

*The giants of the industry have been challenged by the Federal Trade Commission, and it is possible that some of the companies will eventually have to divest themselves of certain products. For the moment, however, the cereal industry remains monopolistic and the public pays much more for every box of cereal than it should.

We find, then, a rather unusual example of an integrated cultural cycle. Competitiveness, which is often cited as a particularly American characteristic, is not only all-pervasive in our culture but also *built into* our cereals. It is absorbed into the body with every spoonful of health-giving breakfast cereal. That's what *Wheaties* means when they say it is the breakfast of champions. *Eating cereals must be seen, then, as a type of communion with the gods of power and success.* Just as cannibals eat the hearts of their victims to get their power, so do do we eat cereals to get the powers of nature and the universe. For as *Team* explains, the Romans ate the same mixture of cereals found in modern *Team* and conquered the world. For fifty cents a box you can do likewise.

# PIZZA: THE SACRAMENT OF THE CITY DWELLER

In the past twenty years pizza seems to have taken America by storm and hundreds of thousands of pizza parlors, palaces, and plazas have opened so that they are now as common as hamburger and chicken stands, those monuments to the iron constitution and lack of discrimination of the American stomach. These pizza joints are the result of the slow, seemingly inevitable movement of pasta from Southern Italy to the tables of the North, and North America in particular. It is not terribly popular in Italy, where it is a "regional" dish. In Milan, where I lived a number of years ago, there are only a few places (that I know about) that serve pizza. So the popularity of pizza in America—and as I understand it, it is now our second most ordered dish—is owing to the triumph of American Italianization. Pizza (and most Italian food served in America) is not "Italian" but an Americanized version of the Southern Italian cooking brought over by the poor immigrants of years gone by. It is the cooking of the poorer classes, the peasants.

Pizza is really a peasant food, and therein lies the secret of its popularity. While it is really only a glorified grilled cheese sandwich, its psychological baggage makes people willing to pay outrageous prices for it. For one thing, we generally can see it being made. In a society in which there is very little "wholeness," in which people have been reduced to being machines (for example, the McDonaldized hamburger-eater), this individual human touch means a great deal. Also, it is something that was made by "mammas." In one pizza parlor I went to there was a short history of pizzas on the menu which told how the Italian mamma makes it for her "delighted bambinos." We all know how important mamma is!

But most important of all, peasant food has somehow become the rage all over the world. Tacos and frijoles are the diet staples for poorer families. In France, high-class people eat cous-cous and pay fancy prices for a wheat dish eaten by the beggars of North Africa. Eating pizza is, in reality, a semi-religious experience. It is a sacrament for the city dweller. Through it he identifies (has communion with) the pre-industrial, pre-urban "good old days" when there was a sense of community and people had, if nothing else, something of an identity.

One can get pizzas now along the sidewalks, in bars, restaurants—almost any place (including supermarkets, where it is often sold in the barbecue section along with the roasted chickens, and in freezers, where it awaits a few minutes in a hot oven). There are even teen-age pizza "nightclubs" which have jazz combos and serve only non-alcoholic beverages—so they are places for good clean fun for the high school set. For the high school kids and college students who go to these places to lift high their steins (of root beer, Seven-Up, etc.) and see "who is going with" whom, the psychological and sacramental aspects of pizza eating are not evident. All they know is that somehow they are leading the good life.

# STYLES, SYMBOLS AND SOCIAL PHENOMENA

## WASHING OUR TIN GODS

When I was growing up in Boston I lived next door to a doctor who spent every Sunday morning cleaning his car. This was before the day of the automatic washers, of course, but even so, it is not anything unusual to see a well-heeled American professional soaping and waxing his car even today.

It seems to be a particularly American phenomenon. One seldom, if ever, sees a middle-class European washing cars.

We might wonder what it is about the American character and psyche that is responsible for such behavior. There are a number of possible explanations.

It may be just one more expression of the "do-it-yourself" individualism which is so much part of our heritage, caused by everything from our frontier experience to the high cost of labor.

It might be something as simple as a desire to keep up the value of one's car, but then, this could just as well be done by having the car washed commercially.

It may also be related to the sense of "workmanship," which finds so little satisfaction in contemporary American society. Most people work at jobs in which they do bits and pieces of something bigger, and so get relatively little sense of satisfaction in this sense. That is one reason why labor insists upon being paid well—the jobs are intrinsically unsatisfying, so they make up for it by insisting upon high monetary compensation.

Washing cars is also a sign of our inherent "classlessness." Although America is not a classless society it tends to believe it is, and to the extent that middle- and upper-middle-class Americans don't feel that much different from other Americans, they are free to wash their cars without betraying their status.

Where I live now, in a fairly well-to-do residential neighborhood in San Francisco, there are a number of men with big, shiny Mercedes cars who are to be seen washing them regularly. Everyone washes his car in America; it is a sign of our free society, and millionaires can do it with just as easy a conscience as lower-middle-class clerks.

Of course cleanliness is a middle-class concept, and those who clean their cars tend to be middle-class. Hippies tend to have flower-decorated dirty junkheaps.

The impulse that emphasizes cleanliness has historic roots in our Puritan experience and is ingrained in our whole bourgeois business culture. Americans who despise "dirty hippies" (the latest acceptable hate figure which has supplanted the "dirty Jews"—though a high percentage of hippies are Jews) also despise dirty cars. But there is a deeper significance, I would argue, to the phenomenon of American car washing, which involves psychic and religious forces. As the American washes and cleans his car he is waging war against the ever-present forces of entropy, the tendency of the universe towards disorder and disintegration.

The American washing his car is like the Dutch boy with his finger in the dike: he is preventing the destruction of his society and ultimately the universe by his actions. This is an extremely personalistic, privatized sense of the way to keep the world going but it happens to be the dominant one in America. That is why the car is such a "love object" here—we may call this *carmour*, car love.

It is also a kind of religious ritual. We know that "cleanliness is next to godliness," and so it is not too far-fetched to see washing cars as functioning in much the way a religious ceremony does. It is a ritual in which the car owner pays obeisance to the god of cars and expresses his love for having been able to "Move up to Mercury" or some other wonder of that sort.

The fact that many cars are named after animals—incorporating their qualities into that of the machine—only adds further evidence to this thesis, for we find the same kind of thing in many primitive religions; it is a kind of animism which is ascribed to mechanical rather than natural objects.

Indeed, we can even see the process of washing a car as similar to that of baptism, in which sins are washed away and man (or his car) is regenerated and purified.

Washing a car, then, is a sacred activity. After the American has "bent his knee" (and elbow) to the god of cars he is ready to bow down to charismatic political leaders promising freeways and surrender his autonomy, though he may be saved by the radicals leading the "Dodge rebellion" or some other revolutionary movement.

# STEREOTYPES AND STOICS

One way of studying countries that has been more or less neglected involves analyzing the significance of their national symbols, stereotypes and seals. The symbols I have in mind, here, are creatures which stand for various countries—such as the American eagle, the Russian bear, or the British bulldog, or various monuments, fictional characters, or buildings (such as The Pentagon) which have taken on a symbolic dimension. A distinction can be made between national *symbols*, which stand for a culture as a whole; *stereotypes*, which crystallize certain aspects of the "national character;" and "sayings" or "epigrams" (which reflect certain philosophical and political beliefs) found on the *seals*, coins and other official publications. The eagle symbolizes the loftiness of our aspirations, our idealism, our vision, our grace and our strength. (It must also be noted that the eagle is a bird of prey and a scavenger, but little is said about that.) The Russian bear suggests other qualities: brute strength, slowness, plodding amiability and the like. The British bulldog represents tenacity, a kind heart beneath a gruff exterior, and a bark worse than his bite. All these animals contain a hint of the truth, but are, really, of little value in understanding their countries, for the very opposite characteristics also apply to each country. The American's "lofty" ambition is often spoken of but seldom realized, the slow-moving Russian has industrialized (at frightful cost, admittedly) in little more than a generation, and the British were not terribly tenacious in keeping their colonies. They did not give the world the spectacle of a rousing colonial war in modern times because they were intelligent enough to see what the outcome would have been.

When dealing with the stereotypes of the various countries, it is important to remember that, as distorted and ridiculous as these stereotypes are, most ordinary people think of foreigners in terms of stereotypes. Most people (because of pop culture, in part) see the American as a rich bourgeois slob who is bossed around by his wife, has silly, spoiled children, and is, himself, infantile. Profiles of national characteristics that have been made by various market research companies give us very specific information about stereotypes. Much of the following material comes from a survey made of characteristics of people in

European countries. People were asked about the qualities that characterized their country and other countries, and gave answers, I suggest, on the basis of the stereotypes I am talking about. The following chart summarizes what people think are the basic characteristics of France, Germany, Britain, Italy and America.*

*Chart I:* NATIONAL CHARACTERISTICS—WHAT OTHERS THINK

| *Country* | *Characteristics* |
| --- | --- |
| United States | Energetic, Pleasure-loving, Gay, Hard-working and Scientific. |
| Britain | Cold and Stiff, Scientific, Disciplined, Conscientious, Hard-working. |
| France | Pleasure-loving, Gay, Amorous, Romantic. |
| Germany | Hard-working, Energetic, Scientific, Disciplined. |
| Italy | Amorous, Gay, Excitable, Pleasure-loving, Hard-working, Romantic. |

These characteristics were chosen from a list of fourteen adjectives which could be used to describe people. I have listed the characteristics in order of frequency of assignation. To see the other side of the coin, what people think of *themselves*, see chart II.

*Chart II:* NATIONAL CHARACTERISTICS—SELF-DESCRIPTIONS

| *Country* | |
| --- | --- |
| United States | Energetic, Pleasure-loving, Gay, Hard-working. |
| Britain | Reliable, Hard-working, Conscientious, Pleasure-loving. |
| France | Pleasure-loving, Hard-working, Gay, Conscientious. |
| Germany | Hard-working, Energetic, Conscientious, Scientific. |
| Italy | Romantic, Amorous, Gay, Hard-working. |

*The following adjectives were used in this survey: Amorous, Cold and Stiff, Conscientious, Disciplined, Energetic, Excitable, Frivolous, Gay, Hard-working, Lazy, Pleasure-loving, Reliable, Romantic, Scientific.

Several things are apparent: every country thinks of itself as hard-working, and, except for the British (who do not see themselves as cold and stiff), *there is strong agreement between the stereotypes people have of themselves and what others have of them.* This may be owing to the widespread nature of popular culture, which feeds on simple similarities and grotesque distortions as a means of creating humor and establishing quick frames of reference. Another important point, of course, is that there is usually a certain tinge of truth in the stereotype—otherwise it would never gain any currency. On the whole, Germans are hard-working. Americans are energetic, and one can find coldness and stiffness among certain classes in Britain. But these stereotypes neglect such matters as the emotionalism of the Germans, the industriousness of the Italians, the bitterness of the French and the friendliness of *most* of the British, which are the other side to the coin. Many people reject the idea of national character, arguing that class, regional and ethnic differences make it impossible to generalize about people. But it seems rather evident that despite the similarities one finds among all people and the differences one finds among the sub-groups and sub-cultures of any given country, there are certain ideals and styles of doing things that are, somehow, typical of countries and particular to them. If the stereotype is a matter, more or less, of hearsay and the national symbol is something which tends to take on a significance, there is no question about the seal. It is the official "representation" of the state and its motto is an explicit statement of American ideals. But what does *E Pluribus Unum* mean? The original conception of "many in one" has become transformed, in one sense, by the acid of American self-centeredness into "one into many and each for himself." This is the individualism that de Tocqueville warned Americans about in *Democracy in America*: Individualism is a mature and calm feeling, which disposes each member of the community to sever himself from the mass of his fellows, to draw apart with his family and friends; so that, after he has thus formed a little circle of his own, he willingly leaves society at large to itself. Selfishness originates in blind instinct: individualism proceeds from erroneous judgment more than from depraved feelings . . .

The consequence of all this is that the Americans are led to believe that they stand alone and that their whole destiny is in their own hands. This is part of the American Dream. However, instead of seeing the American as friendly, generous, and good-natured, as well as rich, uncultivated, and the like, I offer a different portrait of the American: as a stoic, skeptic and cynic.

The American is a *cynic* to the extent that he believes that happiness or right and intelligent living lies in conduct that is *independent of events and factors external to himself*. He repudiates society in the name of self (as if there were only one choice between two diametrical opposites) and withdraws from life. If self-control and independence are the basic attributes of cynicism, who has more self-control (thanks to his Calvinism) or independence (from his Calvinism, the frontier, and other historical factors) than the American? And if the second meaning of cynicism is the "belief that human conduct is motivated wholly by self-interest," who could believe this more than the individualistic American?

The American is a *skeptic* to the extent that he believes *one cannot attain "true knowledge"*; thus his morality is individualistic and his religion is fragmented into two hundred (at least) Protestant sects and no official church. Since the good American doubts (if he's from Missouri he must be "shown"), he is slow to act––except, that is, on the personal level. Thus, the American as "skeptic" is very conservative. Since he can't be sure how bad his society is, and how good any new society might be, he tends to let habit be his guide, and modifies his institutions at a frighteningly slow rate.

And the American is a *stoic* to the extent that he believes that *the virtuous man finds happiness in himself, separates politics from morals and despairing of social reform, turns inward*. He learns to be relatively indifferent about suffering or pain (his Calvinism helps him here by putting his emotions in a straightjacket) and to submit himself to "the law of nature." The good society, for the stoic, is a society of moral people. He has little concern for politics and government and social morality as opposed to individual morality. But letting nature take its course is decidedly conservative. So the American does not act, except on the personal level (where he is prone to violence) and in the business world, though even in this sphere we are often regressive and inept.

There are, of course, strong elements of liberalism and progressivism in America, and, as *Future Shock* suggests, we may be breaking through the wall of conservatism created by our cynicism, skepticism and stoicism. There are outposts of progress, so to speak, where people are experimenting with new lifestyles and new forms of social organization, and even in society at large there are lots of gaps and fissures in the social structure where people can live more or less as they want to.

But behind many of the new social movements and so-called heightened forms of consciousness, which involve rejecting the world or society-at-large (we are urged by some to "tune in, turn on and drop out"), we find the same cynicism, skepticism and stoicism that I have been talking about.

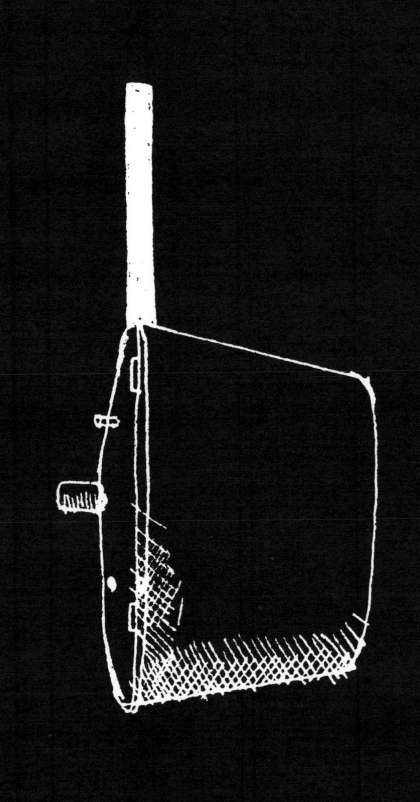

## COOK WHILE TENDER

Life in America is very much like a pressure cooker in terms of the speed with which grown-up concerns become impressed upon young people. Americans tend to sentimentalize youth, perhaps because they tend to deny it to the young. Young Americans are forced to mimic adults, especially in matters of the heart. Socializing between the sexes has been pushed further and further back, and youngsters no longer have the luxury of a few years free of worry about the opposite sex. There was a headline in the papers which graphically illustrates this point. A young boy of eight or ten had a big fight with his father, who refused to give him money to rent a tuxedo for a dance.

American children have no youth. Before they know it they are caught up in the "rat race" of life: they have social girl-boy relationships at a ridiculously early age, and they are led into competitive situations and taught to fight with all they've got in order to win—at all costs. This is done most conspicuously in the notorious Little League, but girls are not slighted: swimming, track, the "wardrobe" competition based on the latest fashion and fad—all unremittingly competitive.

The pressure starts early and never stops. In the college years which are, according to myth, happy and carefree, the pressure is such that we find high suicide rates and a great deal of serious psychological illness. A psychiatrist at the University of Washington noted that within the past decade there has been a great rise in the number of students who are seriously disturbed.

## THE FACE THAT LAUNCHED
## A THOUSAND SHIPS

If you add all the lipsticks, beauty creams and lotions together, you find yourself with about a four-billion-dollar industry. And if you add the beauty parlors to this list, you find beauty a mammoth seven-billion-dollar industry. There's a great deal of money in glamour, obviously, and there always has been. We know that during Cleopatra's day there already existed bleaches, cleansing creams, moisturizers, wrinkle creams, sunburn lotions, dandruff removers, hair dyes, and so forth. And because of woman's quest for beauty a thousand new products were created in the past five years, several hundred of which have succeeded and survived.

According to a recent survey, a typical twenty-year-old working girl spends as much as two-and-a-half hours per day and fifteen dollars per week on being beautiful—or attempting to be so. The most important items are hair products, which are followed by facial care products, which suggests that we have a tendency (or women do, at least) to equate beauty with facial appearance more than with the whole body. Curiously establishments that take care of a woman's hair are called *beauty* parlors, which shows an unconscious identification between hair and beauty. Beautiful hair (which all can have) equals beautiful woman, so all women can be beautiful— even if they are not particularly attractive, as far as their features are concerned. This is what I call "The Medusa Complex." The Medusa was a demon whose hair would make all who looked upon it freeze into stone. The modern would-be Medusa hopes that she too will "knock out" the men who look upon her hair.

*In essence, the process of "making up" and becoming beautiful is a kind of ritual, and is based on a belief in magic.* This magic will help trap a man and lead him into marriage, or help "keep" a married man entranced and endeared. In the first place, there is a kind of formalism involved in making up. (The term itself is very suggestive, implying the creation of something that did not exist before the potions and creams.) The woman assumes, and this is an unconscious process, that because she has used beauty products she must be beautiful, or at least greatly improved. That is, the very act of going through the motions is, in itself, efficacious. In addition to the queer logic of "I use beauty products therefore I am beautiful," there is the belief in

magic, that these potions will transform lead into gold, or enhance whatever beauty one may have. Beauty is not something you have but something you *create*!

And the makeup process has other functions which help alleviate troubled minds. If a girl is not successful on a date—if it doesn't go well—she can blame her cosmetics. It was her cosmetics that "let her down," not any personality deficiency or anything else. If she is married, cosmetics also help by allowing her to create other women of herself. There is a poem about male and female inclinations which is to the point here:

> Higgamus, Hoggamus,
> Women are monogamous,
> Hoggamus, Higgamus,
> Men are polygamous.

A woman, then, becomes many women and "tricks" her husband, thereby enabling him to have variety, and satisfy his polygamous tendencies, and yet keep the home together. Thus, by practicing her black magic, one woman becomes a thousand women and enchants her husband—who, thanks to the recent development of male cosmetics, can also become a thousand men. Cosmetics also allow women to defy Father Time and become immortal—ageless and forever young. And when cosmetics can no longer stem the tide there is cosmetic surgery, and other fabulous and secret operations and magic rituals exist for more serious problems.

Phyllis Diller had cosmetic surgery and emerged considerably more attractive than she used to look. Before the surgery she had a face that would launch a thousand ships—but in the opposite direction, as she used to put it. It will be interesting to see what effect her new face will have on her career, which was based on her being an "ugly housewife" type.

# THE SUBVERSIVE *"HE"*—
# A STUDY IN MALE DOMINATION

There has been a lot of agitation at California State University, San Francico, by women upset about their state of relative deprivation in American culture. They put out a brochure suggesting that "Women are people," in which they lamented that many see them as " different species" (chicks, cows, pigs), "something good to eat" (cookies, tarts, tomatoes), "mindless sex objects" (teases, sexpots) or "anything but people" (babies, dears, hags, broads, dolls), etc. They quoted several radical thinkers on the rights of women. They also supplied abundant statistics to demonstrate that women are continually discriminated against and are in a clearly intolerable situation. As one college-educated girl said, ". . . when I need to go to the drugstore to buy some more Pampers, that's a big thing. I plan my whole day around it."

When I read this handout, in which they spelled emancipated e-mancipated, a thought struck me—that there is not only discrimination in our laws and society but also that women are subjected to an insidious, almost invisible domination in the very language they use to think about themselves and argue for their rights. *There is a subversive "he" in the English language that has an almost subliminal dominating impact on the female psyche.* Almost everyplace you look there is a "he" or "man" or "male"—even in such common terms as she, woman and female. (Jung explains the he in the she as the *animus* and the she in the he as the *anima,* both of which must overcome for true sexual identity and maturity to be achieved.)

But the cases I've mentioned above are quite obvious. What about some of the more insidious examples. Why Manishevitz matsoh and not Womanishevitz? Why manuals? What about romantic, command, malediction, manufacture, manager, shaman? Why heman and not sheman? Why hedonist and not shedonist? Why Hebrew and not Shebrew? Why Hearse and not Shearse? Why heel and not sheel? Why heart and blaspheme? Why heinous and not sheinous? Women have almost no terms for themselves without some reference to the dominant male intruding: woman, female, her, she, women, heroine. This must have some kind of an effect upon women, especially if the "Law of Primacy" (which states that first things tend to shape second things) holds.

# THE MOTEL:
## Home Away From Home
## In the Plastic Society

The "motel" is the biggest new thing in the American travel scene—that is, that part of it dealing with putting people up for a night or so. In 1940, for example, there were 13,000 motels with a total of 160,000 rooms in America and in 1965 there were 43,000 motels with more than a million rooms. The growth of motels has truly been, in the best American tradition, phenomenal. And the motel started poor—from poor but honest parentage: the cabins of the Depression years. But these cabins have taken on a new form, indeed: to a great degree the motels symbolize and epitomize that which is vulgar, ostentatious and monstrous—what we now call "plastic," in American life. But what is the real significance of the motel and how is the motel different from the hotel? These are questions which must be answered to understand the cultural meaning of the motel.

The word "hotel" is derived from the "hôtes" of medieval Europe. As Henri Pirenne tells us in *Economic and Social History of Medieval Europe*:

*The term* hôtes *(literally "guests"), which appears more and more frequently from the beginning of the twelfth century, is characteristic of the movement which was going on in rural society. As the name indicates, the* hôte *was a new-comer, a stranger.*

A hotel, then, is a place for strange *people,* and to parallel this, the motel is a place for strange *cars.* The motel is one more extension of the automobile in American culture and a manifestation of the superiority of the car. Of course, most people are not conscious of this, but I can't help but think that much of the frenzy and extravagance we find in the newer super-deluxe motels is an attempt to soothe wounded human psyches over their status inferiority.

Even the definition of the motel, as found in *Webster's Seventh New Collegiate Dictionary,* is suggestive:

*MOTEL: (blend of motorist and hotel): a building or group of buildings used as a hotel in which the rooms are directly accessible from an outdoor parking area.*

The necessity of proximity of the motel bedroom is one more example of that "individualism" so characteristic of American culture: every American in his Holiday Inn sleeps contentedly just a stone's throw from his Mustang.

The motel is a great success story in the classic American rags-to-riches style. The motel room which used to average $4.20 in 1925 cost $12.00 in 1965 and even more now. Actually, the motels have been lucky; they were there when the age of the car exploded upon the American people. It is known, for example, that 85 percent of people taking hotel and motel rooms arrive by car, and just as the car has revolutionized grocery shopping (with the supermarket and parking lot) and banking and everything else, it has revolutionized hotels.

Hotels also tend to be urban, in the middle of cities, and as the cities die from the center outward, the hotels feel the pressure. What has happened lately, of course, is that all new hotels provide parking space, so that now it is often hard to distinguish between a hotel (with parking space) and a motel, especially now that motels are rising higher and higher off the ground. It is significant, however, that between 1940 and 1960, some 5,000 hotels went out of business, though the new, larger hotels have managed to keep the number of hotel rooms available at about the same level.

One other thing must be mentioned: the general uniformity of motel rooms. There are numerous motifs used in motels but, most of them, being new, are modern. What you find, then, is a rather crushing sameness—so that you have the sense of not having really gone anywhere since the last chrome and neon, swimming-pooled place you were at.

The following chart shows the essential differences between motels and hotels:

HOTELS AND MOTELS

|  | *Hotel* | *Motel* |
|---|---|---|
| origin | 12th C. | mid-20th C. |
| for | people | cars |
| nature | communal | individualistic |
| location | urban | suburban, then urban |
| services | bellhops, etc. | bring your own |
| occupancy | 60% | 75% |

The growth and success of the motels are further testimony to the supremacy of the automobile in American culture. The motel, of course, really exists for the *motorist*, but what is a motorist? One who drives a car! Even here the machine seems dominant. It would not be too farfetched to say that America will truly be a great country when it learns to treat its people as well as it treats its automobiles.

But this, of course, is wishful thinking.

## BROADLOOM RUGS

The broadloom rug is, I think, a very fitting symbol of the fact that "consumption" is no longer the luxury of the rich. Now the middle classes (and lower classes, too) can consume things that were once "beyond them." There is much talk by sociologists and others about America being a "consumer" culture. It is asserted that once it was a producer culture, in keeping with its Puritan ethos, but that this has been abandoned—and Americans are consumer crazy. They are taught from infancy to consume, and to consume everything from sex to silverplate.

I would not dispute that there is much that is overdone and somewhat grotesque about the frenzy of American consuming, but what is a country supposed to do that produces with such abandon? After all, consuming is only a function of producing, and the American who works like a demon to produce MUST work like a demon to consume. Americans are not the only consumers. The wealthy classes in all countries consume—and extravagantly. But it is vulgar and ostentatious for the American middle classes to load themselves up with rugs and refrigerators, but in good taste for rich Englishmen to buy Rolls Royces.

## AMERICAR THE BEAUTIFUL:
### The Automobile as Love Object
### and Symbol of The American Dream

I often have a fantasy about America in the year 2000. By then, my fantasy tells me, we will have produced so many automobiles in America that in certain cities there will be no room left to drive them. Automobiles will be delivered by helicopter and placed in front of, or near, a purchaser's residence, and all he will be able to do is wax and clean his car from time to time and sit in it. This is because our space is limited and our capacity to produce automobiles is unlimited. This nightmare will never come true because, finally, after an all-consuming love affair with the automobile, we are beginning to wake up and see reality. The honeymoon is over, and we are now starting to recognize the psychic and social cost of our reliance upon the automobile as our principal mode of transportation. Some 50,000 persons are killed and hundreds of thousands are injured every year in automobile accidents; and smog, noise pollution and countless other horrors emanating from an excess of automobiles are becoming apparent every day.

By now, of course, the automobile is so much a part of our culture that it will take some rather remarkable measures to escape from its dominance. We have drive-in restaurants, movies, mortuaries, banks and almost anything else you can think of. One reason cities are dying is a lack of parking space for workers and shoppers. Because we do not have adequate mass transportation facilities, any store or institution that cannot supply parking space (a very expensive commodity in cities, where a parking stall in a garage may be worth $20,000) is doomed.

About one out of six workers in America has a job that is directly or indirectly connected with the automobile industry—or auxiliary industries such as gasoline or tires. The automobile dominates us economically as well as physically, and has affected the pattern of our housing (the suburb), consumption (the shopping center), and even our sense of who we are in the world—and where we are going. We talk of "four-wheel personalities" and, until recently, so I understand, many girls were reluctant to go out on dates with young men who didn't have cars, and, in some cases, the "right" kind of cars. For some people, cars are not only status symbols but actually love objects in themselves, with glamor, raciness and other lovable characteristics.

And automobile racing, statistics show, is now our most popular spectator sport. We have created all kinds of bizarre car sports, from the Indianapolis 500 to drag races and demolition derbies—orgies of destruction in which old hulks batter one another in a modern manifestation of the gladiatorial battles of ancient Rome. It may be that we have replaced *charisma*, a kind of personal grace and spirit found in some people, with *carisma*, a status and personality-type (the "Mustang mentality," for instance) gained by purchasing a specific model of car, and having nothing to do with personal characteristics or abilities.

There are any number of reasons for our preoccupation with the automobile. We are a nation of so-called individualists, and the automobile is the ultimate means of individual mobility—though it is also the most costly. The freedom and sense of power we feel when driving are particularly important to young people, who find the automobile and motorized speed both a means of escape from social restrictions and an exhilarating, thrilling experience in its own right. But the matter of mobility is a complicated one, for not only does it involve getting from place to place, but also—especially in America—it involves social mobility.

The term "social mobility" refers to rising in the world in the best Horatio Alger tradition. But there is a big question about how possible it is to rise in contemporary America—that is, in a significant manner. And some have suggested that, in effect, mobility is now blocked. In the old days it was possible for office boys to become corporation presidents; nowadays one needs a graduate degree from an important business school (Harvard, Wharton School of Finance, etc.) to start off decently in the corporation hierarchies, and a good start is most of the battle. As Seymour Martin Lipset points out in *Political Man*, "The most recent data indicate that *actual* social mobility in Europe is as high as it is in the United States but the *belief* in mobility differs." America, which prides itself as being uniquely "a land of opportunity" offers little more than Europe does to the upward bound citizen, though it claims to offer a great deal more. After all, every American is taught that he can be President of the United States but it seems necessary to be a millionaire to try (at least in recent years).

Because of the contradictions between the ideal of rising in the world and the fact that we seldom rise as fast or as far as we were led to believe we could, the ordinary American feels frustrated. He is an engine revved up to rise and he cannot. What can he do? The answer is obvious—he can move laterally, and that is what he does. I will use the term *lateral mobility* to cover this phenomenon. Lateral mobility is a functional alternative to social vertical mobility: those who cannot move *high* in corporate structures can move *fast*—on the streets. Lateral mobility manifests itself in automobile driving in what is called "the quick getaway." The ability of cars to accelerate rapidly (after they have stopped  for a Stop sign or a red light and before they stop again, one block down the road) is an important selling feature in cars. Automobiles come with enormous engines for precisely this reason—so people can zoom away, get places before others, and therefore "succeed" in a kind of competition, though it leads to no results of any significance—except crashes and crumpled fenders. The automobile gives the poor status-frustrated American an opportunity to show how masterful he is, though his race towards no place in an ever receding horizon is doomed to failure.*

In a sense there is a crazy parallel between the accelerating driver and the rising executive in America. Success in America is always relative, it has no bounds to speak of—you can never rest and consider yourself to have arrived, for the law of competition tells you there is no standing still. Thus corporation executives work themselves to death with amazing zeal in America, since their culture has told them they can never stop in their pursuit of wealth and status. In a similar manner, the poor American driver (whose social mobility has been blocked) works off his frustrations by racing hell-bent to the next Stop sign. Sartre said, "Hell is other people." For the American, however, it is the rush hour.

---

*There may be an inverse correlation between a person's sense of "self" and the size of the engine in his car. People who feel petty and insignificant, for whatever reason, may need gigantic V-8s, and people who feel weak may need "muscle" cars. Choosing options for cars may be one of the few ways left in which individuals can make decisions that count, and for many it is the only means at their disposal for displaying creativity, as well as status.

# WHAT'S BUGGING THE AFFORDINARY MAN

There is a great deal of talk nowadays about "the little man," about all the mute people who make up some kind of a silent majority that is disturbed or perhaps even alienated. Polls show that large numbers of people are leading lives of "quiet desperation" for one reason or another. Many people have jobs that are unsatisfying. Others have trouble with their children and still others have sexual hangups, alcohol or drug problems, etc. Some poor souls have compounds of most or all of these afflictions.

We no longer are willing to suffer in silence as Job did. In the story of Job the Lord says to Satan:

Hast thou considered my servant Job?
For there is none like him in the earth,
A perfect and upright man,
One that feareth God and escheweth evil:
And he still holdeth fast his integrity,
Although thou movedst me against him
To destroy him without cause.

*Without cause!* Maybe that's the problem the ordinary guy faces. Something is wrong but he can't quite put his finger on it. What's bugging him, anyway?

What has happened is that he has become a victim of a culture that has lost sight of personal and humane values and which now measures everyone against one standard: "How much money do you make?" *The ordinary man has become the "affordinary man," a person whose only distinction is what he can afford. (Afford: to be able to bear the cost of without serious loss or detriment)*

All of our distinctions—a sense of humor, courage, honesty, kindness —have all been reduced to one category: consumption. Being "able" has been replaced by being "able to afford," and the ironic thing is that we have been taught to measure our progress (affordinancy) by our dehumanization. Human relationships have been subordinated to object gathering, and the bigger your pile of gadgets, cars, credit cards and bills, the more "successful" you count yourself.

This is a function of our equalitarian society, in which there are no official or legal class distinctions. We do not have a hereditary aristocracy (*aristoi* means best) and so the only way a person can show he has "made it" is by conspicuous consumption. You are what you can afford, so to speak, and everyone has an equal chance, so legend tells us.

But though we do not have an official aristocracy, we do have one. It is not social but *economic*, and those in the highest stratum of society, a bare one percent of the population, lead relatively private and privileged lives, so that our economic aristocracy becomes, in effect, a social one also. But it is not legal or official, so that many Americans delude themselves into thinking that we have no classes. Although there are some opportunities for moving up in our society, those at the top start out way ahead, and very few are able to catch them.

Since we measure achievement in economic terms, this means those at the bottom must suffer from a grievous sense of inadequacy. In order to assuage these feelings, the affordinary man goes into debt, and a gigantic economic institution has developed to allow him to do so—installment buying. Figures show that the ordinary man is heavily in debt, which puts terrific emotional strains on him.

He is caught in a tragic dilemma. If he doesn't get the various things that advertising and cultural pressure have made him feel he needs, he does not feel successful. But if he goes into debt to get them, he faces the problem of paying for everything on a budget that is often too small. He becomes sucked into the position of being a debtor— paying interest on installment purchases and interest on loans he takes out to meet the installment payments.

What makes the situation worse is that the affordinary man never really *owns* things—he is always paying for them. And things never really have a price, since the only consideration for the affordinary man is "how much per *month?*"

Nothing really means anything! Everything is fragmentary: he pays installments on things he doesn't really own but just uses (so to speak), for which there is no real price, only the monthly charge. Caught up in such a situation how can a person be anything more than fragmentary himself? Is it not possible that one thing bugging the affordinary man is that he doesn't have any sense of completeness,

of being a whole person, because he is so submerged in fragmentary things and operations? This situation is often compounded when a person does work that is trivial and brutalizing, such as working on an assembly line and repeating the same operation every 32 seconds eight hours a day.

For this terrible and unsatisfying work in which most affordinary men are caught there is only one reward—money—with which you can buy (in theory) things and, so to speak, redeem yourself by piling up "junk" which shows *how* you are doing, since *who* you are is irrelevant now.

Unfortunately even this escape, consumption, becomes boring and unsatisfying. The affordinary man has *nothing*. He can't compete with the rich in consuming, and then becomes, by definition, some kind of an inferior being. What he can consume eventually becomes less satisfying, and more often than not, he becomes so debt plagued that he suffers from destructive nervous strain. This is compounded during times of unemployment when he can be laid off. Since talent, character, and other human values have come subordinated, there is nothing left.

All of this deals with the majority of Americans who are narrowly keeping themselves above poverty. What about the millions of Americans who live *in* poverty and don't even have enough to eat? The affordinary man who works hard for what little he gets becomes enraged when he sees money, "his money," he believes, going to the poor. The affordinary man, the average guy working for a living, and the poor make up perhaps sixty percent of the population. Those who are not physically impoverished are psychologically impoverished, and many are both, in this grouping. It is a sad commentary on the richest country in the world that such large numbers of people are so distressed.

We might look at "affordinancy" as a religion of sorts. Ordination occurs when a person gets his charge account, credit card, and check book. We worship at supermarkets and department stores, the cathedrals of consumption of modern man. (In this respect, it is most significant that Sears will build the tallest building in the world.) We "sin" by getting behind in our payments and we are "redeemed" by

getting a loan from a bank or loan company. But it is a mockery of a religion that has been described and it leaves us unsatisfied and in great despair.

Revising our economic system to bring everyone out of poverty is not enough. We must somehow do away with the forces in our culture that lead people to see themselves in terms of what they can afford, and only that. Leaving people at the mercy of a consumption society, to feel miserable if they are not surrounded by goods of all sorts, and the various junk of our society, is the one thing we cannot, as a society, afford.

AND SO WE LEAVE OUR FRIENDS DANGLING IN A WEB FAR MORE POWERFUL THAN ANY WHICH *SPIDER-MAN* CAN WEAVE -- THE MYSTERIOUS, DRAMATIC WEB OF *FATE!* NEXT ISSUE WE WILL MEET A GREAT NEW VILLAIN -- FIND MORE SPECTACULAR THRILLS -- AS *SPIDER-MAN* DISCOVERS THE STRANGE SECRET OF BETTY BRANT!

THE END
...FOR NOW!

Here are some ideas to think about, topics to consider for discussion and investigation, books to read, and other matters dealing with popular culture and American society. The purpose of this material is to help you "come to grips," so to speak, with popular culture, by raising some questions, offering some speculations and noting some further reading. I hope that this appendix will help you apply what you have learned in this book to your own experiences.

That is, after all, what we mean by *relevant—information that has a direct bearing upon our lives, that is immediate.* As you think about the material in the book and in this appendix there should be some kind of a "shock of recognition." Hopefully you will see that many of the essays involve matters that have been an intimate part of your own experience, and it may be that some of the notions floating around in your head in some way have been "put there" by popular culture. If this book has helped you learn how you have arrived at yourself—created, for better or worse, an "identity"—I feel my efforts have been well spent.

## Questions and Considerations about Pop Culture in General

1. Why is popular culture so unpopular with some people (certain educators, literary critics, self-appointed guardians of our taste, etc.) ?

2. Following are some of the criticisms made of popular culture. Evaluate each of the critiques in terms of your own experiences, specific examples of pop culture that support the criticism (or cause you to disagree with it) , and decide whether or not the critics are seizing upon the worst examples of a given kind of popular culture, and not representative examples.

### Attacks on Pop Culture:

It promotes escapism.

It is a narcotic and leads to addiction (especially TV) .

It must be vulgar, appealing to the lowest common denominator.

It homogenizes our culture—destroys regional culture.

It trivializes—makes everything stupid and monotonous.

It promotes passivity.

It distracts us from serious concerns such as the need for social change.

It isolates people from one another.

It is sentimental—drips with emotion.

It is too violent.

It distorts life—gives us a false picture of reality.

It is sensationalistic—appeals to emotions rather than reason.

It is simplistic—obsessed with a narrow range of themes (such as sex, death and violence).

It is based on formulas and reduces everything so it can fit in some formula.

It is seductive, and debases sexuality for commercial exploitation.

It uses stereotypes.

It arouses anxieties but does not give us satisfaction and release from them.

3. Do you think that it is correct to make a distinction between popular culture and "high" culture? If *Hamlet* is shown on television, is that high culture or popular culture? Is unpopular culture the opposite of popular culture, and if something is not popular does that mean it is "good"?

4. Can you think of any ideas, notions, or expectations about life which you got from popular culture? Can you narrow this down and find a particular example (a song or television program or movie) which was in any way responsible for your ideas and expectations, your view of yourself or your sense of your possibilities?

5. What changes in pop culture have you noticed? How important have they been? What do you think they tell us about American society? Answer this question by examining *specific* aspects of pop culture, such as advertising, kinds of heroes in television and the movies, jokes made by comedians, and that kind of thing.

### Questions and Considerations about Specific Kinds of Pop Culture
### Amusements and Entertainments

1. How well do the three basic aspects of comic strips and comic books—the *art work*, the *language*, and the *narrative structure*—relate to one another? When you examine the art work, consider

the following: features of characters, proportions, age of heroes and villains, stereotypes used, rendering of technology, landscapes, women, the way violence is represented, the crudity or sophistication of the art work in general and the significance of various kinds of gesture.

When you examine the use of language, take the following into account: alliteration, irony, allusions to famous people and events, verb tenses, humor, names, values espoused, tone, and make-up words to represent violence, blows, etc.

When you examine the structure of comics, consider: the length of each tale, action, plot, development, use of flashbacks, rendering of character, motivation, conflict, and resolutions.

2. What are your favorite comic strips? Why? Do you still read comic books? If so, which ones? What do you like about them? Have you noticed any *changes* in comic books over the past few years? Why do you think people read the comics?

3. What are the *major goals* of the various comic strip and comic book characters (safety, security, wealth, thrill, power, love, fame, popularity, knowledge, revenge, etc.) and what *means* do they use to achieve these goals (violence, trickery, hard work, charm, etc.)? Are those characters different, in these respects, from most people?

4. Some sociologists have suggested that heroes (whether in comics or any other kind of pop culture) do the following things for their readers or followers: provide *vicarious experiences*, create new *roles*, and help towards developing new *selves*—new identities. Take some comic strip or comic book heroes and analyze them in terms of these functions. What conclusions do you reach? Do the same with heroic figures from certain movies and television programs.

5. Is a hero someone who *reflects* his society's values (a first among equals, so to speak) or someone who transforms and *shapes* his society's values? What significance do you attribute to the fact that lone heroes have been replaced by groups of heroes or teams? Who are your heroes? Why do you think they are heroic? What do your heroes tell us about American culture? Yourself?

6. Some people make a distinction between "art" and "entertain-

ment." Art (novels, theatre, poetry, etc.) supposedly "frees" us, lifts repressions, moves us emotionally and helps us "master reality." Entertainment (television, sports, popular fiction, etc.) supposedly leads to shallow contentment, offers cheap thrills and escapism, but doesn't give us any insights into life. Do you think this distinction is valid? Can entertainment be art? Can art be entertaining? Take some specific television programs or detective stories and analyze them in terms of the notions listed under art and entertainment. Do you think the distinction holds up?

7. What is a situation comedy? Are there kinds of comedies which are not situational? What significance do you attribute to the lack of a mother or a father in many of the recent situation comedies? Situation comedies are reliant, to a great degree, on stereotypes. What significance does this have?

8. Try making up a situation comedy of your own. Write a proposal describing the various characters and the basic theme of the comedy. Cast it with specific actors and actresses. Can you think of any fresh and interesting situations, or have all the situations been used up?

9. There are a number of reasons that have been put forth to explain the popularity of sports with the general public. These include: a kind of heroism is possible; sports provide an interesting topic for discussion; sports are a diversion, a way of recapturing youth, of escaping from problems of the real world; the violence in some sports allows us to discharge tensions and pent-up aggressive emotions; sports are the moral equivalent of war; and betting on sports allows risk-taking with relatively minor consequences. Can you think of any other reasons sports are popular? Take a sport and analyze it in terms of the ideas given above. Compare two sports—such as baseball and football. Do you have any explanations for pro football's rise in popularity?

10. Take some form of entertainment and analyze it in terms of its function for its audience, the social class and age group it primarily appeals to, and what it reflects about our society. Try to note changes and new developments that have taken place in various entertainment forms—for example, from strip-tease to the

topless, from Tin Pan Alley popular music to rock and folk, from Puritanical films to ones which are very explicit about sexual matters. Do the various developments mentioned above add up to a move towards realism and sophistication or exploitation and crude sensationalism?

11. Make a list of our basic stereotypes. What functions do they serve? Do we have any new stereotypes to add to our old ones? How do we avoid stereotyping? Should we?

## Getting the Message

1. How does advertising work? Do most ads appeal primarily to our rationality or to our emotions? Is this good or bad?

2. What view of the world does advertising foster? Does it simplify things? Focus only upon certain class levels? Does it give us expectations which are unrealistic?

3. What about the visceral impact of television ads upon us? What *techniques* are used in commercials to affect our behavior, stir our emotions and desires?

4. What basic motivations are found in commercials? What appeals are made? Are they constructive or destructive?

5. How truthful are advertisements? Does advertising lead to a general cynicism and distrust in people? If so, what impact might this have on society?

6. What interesting social considerations can you find in advertising? Take some specific advertisements or television commercials (the latter are the most important form of advertisement now) and analyze them in terms of the questions asked above and some of the following considerations: roles given to women, use of racial minorities, symbolic rewards and gratifications shown as important, and emphasis on consumermania as a way of gaining happiness.

7. In your analysis of advertising and society, also do the following: analyze the artistic quality of the ad or ads; explain how the ads relate to social, cultural and economic matters; and discuss the significance of the *product* being advertised. It is frequently possible to relate advertisements to ideas about American culture and

society found in the writings of anthropologists, psychologists, and sociologists. For example, many social scientists have written about such topics as our youth culture, the generation gap, and conditional love (love offered as a reward for doing certain things and withdrawn as a punishment at other times). Do you find any of these concepts useful in interpreting advertisements? Can you think of any other concepts which might be used for this kind of thing?

8. It is frequently possible to distinguish between the *informational* content of an advertisement and the *psychological* barrage included which attempts to influence behavior—that is, get you to buy the product. Take some ads and separate the information from the various appeals. Try this with ads for automobiles, gas, cigarettes, beer, cosmetics, foods, appliances, etc. What do you find?

9. Examine, with care, some of the printed matter that you come across during the course of an ordinary day. Look critically at such things as the type styles used, the amount of "white space" left around the type, the quality of the paper used, and the language. What differences do you notice between newspapers and magazines in general? How do different organizations convey impressions about themselves in newspaper advertisements? How much information about life do you get from reading real estate ads and help wanted ads? What picture of the world do these ads (and others) convey?

10. Write a "Situation Wanted" advertisement for yourself. Do you find it difficult? Depressing?

11. Take a newspaper and see how much space (in column inches) is devoted to advertising, light news (or entertainment) and hard news. Do the same with some magazines. What do you find? On the basis of this information, what conclusions do you reach about the functions of newspapers and magazines—or, at least, the particular newspapers and magazines you have examined?

12. Assume that you had a million dollars to be spent in producing a magazine. Make up a "dummy" of this magazine, with a title and proposed table of contents. Write an advertisement to be sent to

possible readers explaining why you created the magazine and why they should subscribe to it.

## Common Objects and Everyday Activities

1. Certain artifacts—common objects showing human design and workmanship—seem to have special psychological and social significance. If you were an archaeologist and had to figure out or *derive* our society from some of our ordinary, simple objects, what objects would you choose and how would you go about "reading" or analyzing the objects? (If archaeologists can learn a great deal about ancient societies from remains of pots, coins and such things, we can do the same kind of thing. As Ernest Dichter said in his *Handbook of Consumer Motivations,* "The objects which surround us do not simply have utilitarian aspects; rather, they serve as a kind of mirror which reflects our own image. Objects which surround us permit us to discover more and more of ourselves . . . In a sense, therefore, the knowledge of the soul of things is possibly a very direct and new and revolutionary way of discovering the soul of man.")

2. Your basic concern in investigating artifacts should be in discovering their social and psychological significance. Suppose you are investigating a cigarette lighter. You might ask yourself the following questions: what is its function or basic purpose? Does it have a hidden significance, which we are not conscious of? What basic values does it reflect? (Some you might think about are: fascination with gadgets? need for certainty? sense of power? sense of sexual potency? need for speed and efficiency?) How has it changed over the years? Does it appeal to specific classes and social strata? For this latter question, it might be wise to discuss a a specific brand of cigarette lighter and compare it with other brands.

3. Make a list of some of the artifacts that you have and see if you can discern what significance they have for you. Think, for example, about some of the simple appliances in your home, or the foods you eat, the clothes you wear, and that kind of thing. Give the list to someone who doesn't know you very well and ask him

to "psychoanalyze" the list and tell him what kind of a person is "behind" it.

4. Suppose the government asked you to fill up a large space capsule which was to represent American culture at the present time and give future generations an idea (some hundreds or thousands of years hence) of what life was like in the seventies. What would you put in the capsule? Justify *each* choice.

## Styles, Symbols and Social Phenomena

1. According to *Webster's Seventh New Collegiate Dictionary,* style is "a mode of expressing thought in language; *esp*: a manner of expression characteristic of an individual, period, school, or nation." If we broaden this definition and include not only language but clothing, hair, makeup and other kinds of expression, it is obvious that we have a valuable tool for getting interesting insights into individuals, periods and societies. Take some article of clothing such as shoes or stockings and trace the way it has changed over the past thirty years. Do the same with cosmetics and hairstyles and any other kind of stylistic expression you find interesting. What do you discover?

2. There is a much debated theory that we are moving towards *unisex*—that supposedly "male" characteristics and styles are being feminized, and supposedly "female" characteristics are becoming more masculine. Does an analysis of styles lead you to agree with the unisex hypothesis? What specifically would lead you to discount the unisex hypothesis?

3. What is the relationship between social class and styles? Some styles come from the bottom and move up and other styles seem to move from the top downwards. Give some specific examples of each.

4. What is the significance of hippie clothing styles and life styles? What is a hippie? How do you differentiate between real hippies and weekend hippies? Is there anything wrong with being a weekend hippie? Why are you hearing less and less about hippies?

5. What are the basic clothing styles that are popular now? Why are they popular? What do they tell us about our society? Is it possible

that many people use clothing and hair to express themselves because they have no other way of expressing themselves?

6. Why do some styles catch on and others fail? Why did the "midi" bomb? Why were the mini and micro-mini so popular? Do you feel "left out" if you don't keep up with the latest fashions? Do you feel that you are "exploited" by the clothing and cosmetic industries, which continually change styles, or do you think it is just a matter of individual choice and you are free to do whatever you want to do?

7. Do you think that some of the recent social phenomena such as student rebellions and women's liberation are "fads" or serious social movements? What is a "fad"? How does it get started? Is it possible that social movements can also have a faddist aspect to them? Can a social movement become pop culture? Are social movements, such as women's liberation, related in any way to pop culture? Caused by pop culture?

8. What role do cars play in your life? Do you think you are "dominated" by car culture here in America? If so, explain how. If not, explain how you have escaped its clutches. What additions can you make to the list of areas of life (discussed in the essay on cars) which have been affected by cars?

9. Take some theme or general notion, such as "generation conflict" or "the battle of the sexes" or "technology" or "success" and find manifestations of this notion in advertisements, jokes, movies, styles and various other forms of popular culture. Put them into a notebook and write a brief introduction explaining the importance of the theme, its social and psychological significance, and why you chose each of the items in the notebook.

10. Here are a number of topics for discussion and investigation:

| | |
|---|---|
| Tall tales | Comedians: Benny, Sahl, Bruce, Hope, etc. |
| American fools | Negro humorists |
| American mythology | Graffiti |
| Black humor | Joke cycles: elephant, grape, Polish, etc. |
| Jewish humor | |

Dirty jokes
Children's humor
The cowboy as culture hero
The detective as culture hero
The secret agent as culture hero
New American art forms
Vernacular art forms
Teen culture

Posters
Billboards
Package labels
Package design: bottles, etc.
Dance styles: evolution of . . .
Franchises and fast foods
Cinema
Sports: football, baseball, hockey, etc.
Games: *Monopoly, Sorry,* etc.
Body decoration
Hair styles
Greeting cards
Political ads: selling candidates
Medicines, beauty aids, etc.
Columnists in papers
Uniforms
Images in media: of the businessman, the professor, etc.
Bathroom design

Popular children's literature: Nancy Drew, etc.

Pop art
Fashions: clothing, shoes
Appeals and themes in advertising
Pulp magazines
Comics (strips, books)
Radio programs and heroes
Television programs and heroes
Situation comedies
Specific TV programs
Kitchen utensils

Fads, crazes, etc.
Supermarkets, department stores
Status symbols
Popular music, rock, etc.
Popular literature: best sellers
Gossip columns
Advice columns
Classified ads
Underground papers, etc.
Radio talk shows
The rhetoric of menus, ads, etc.
Foods, snacks, etc.
Eating patterns

Kitchen design
Electrical appliances
Creation of stars: Nancy Sinatra, etc.
Fan magazines

Female comedians: problems, etc.
Formulas in TV programs, movies, etc.
Science fiction
Drinks: popularity of Scotch
Common objects: telephone, can opener, electric knife, etc.
Motorcycle styles
Views of the good life in media, ads, etc.
Musical comedy and theatre

New religions and collective behavior
The ten-speed bicycle
Toys
Signs
Popular logic
Circuses
Rodeos
Topless, bottomless and strip-tease
Organic food
Pop, wine
Hamburger stands

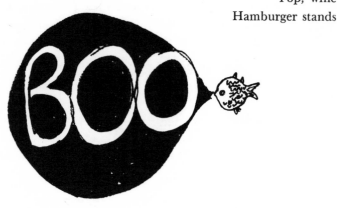

# POP CULTURE BIBLIOGRAPHY

Agee, James, **Agee on Film,** Ivan Oblensky, 1958.

Allen, Dick, ed., **Science Fiction: The Future,** Harcourt, Brace, Jovanovich, 1971.

Allen, Don, **The Electric Humanities,** Pflaum, 1971.

Amis, Kingsley, **New Maps of Hell: A Survey of Science Fiction,** Harcourt, Brace, 1960.

    **The James Bond Dossier,** New American Library, 1965.

Arbuthnot, May Hill, **Children's Reading in the Home,** Scott, Foresman & Co., 1969.

    **Children and Books,** Scott, Foresman & Co., 1964.

Arlen, Michael J., **The Living Room War,** Viking, 1969.

Arnheim, Rudolph, **Film as Art,** University of California Press, 1957.

Baker, Stephen, **Visual Persuasion,** McGraw-Hill, 1961.

Barzun, Jacques and Wendell H. Taylor, **Catalogue of Crime: Being a Reader's Guide to the Literature of Mystery, Detection and Related Genres,** Harper & Row, 1961.

Bazin, André, **What is Cinema?,** Vol. 1, University of California Press, 1967, Vol. 2, 1971.

Becker, Stephen, **Comic Art in America,** Simon & Schuster, 1959.

Berger, Arthur Asa, **Li'l Abner: A Study in American Satire,** Twayne, 1970.

Buzzi, Giancarlo, **Advertising: Its Cultural and Political Effects,** University of Minnesota Press, 1967.

Cantor, Norman F., and Michael S. Werthman, **The History of Popular Culture** (2 vols.) , Macmillan, 1968.

Cantril, Hadley, **The Invasion from Mars: A Study in the Psychology of Panic,** Harper Torchbook, 1966.

Carpenter, Edmund, and Marshall McLuhan, eds., **Explorations in Communication,** Beacon, 1960.

Casty, Alan, ed., **Mass Media and Mass Man,** Holt, Rinehart & Winston, 1968.

Cawelti, John G., **The Six-Gun Mystique,** Bowling Green University Popular Press, 1971.

Cole, Barry, ed., **Television: Selections from TV Guide Magazine,** Free Press, 1970.

Couperie, Pierre, and Maurice C. Horn, **A History of the Comic Strip,** Crown, 1968.

Crews, Frederick C., **The Pooh Perplex,** E. P. Dutton, 1963.

Crist, Judith, **The Private Eye, the Cowboy and the Very Naked Girl: Movies from Cleo to Clyde,** Holt, Rinehart & Winston, 1968.

Cross, Jennifer, **The Supermarket Trap: The Consumer and the Food Industry,** Indiana University Press, 1970.

Daniels, Les, **Comix: A History of Comic Books in America,** Outerbridge & Dienstfrey, 1971.

Davies, Hunter, **The Beatles,** McGraw-Hill, 1968 (Dell, 1969).

Deer, Irving, and Harriet A. Deer, **The Popular Arts: A Critical Reader,** Scribners, 1967.

Deford, Frank, **Five Strides on the Banked Track: The Life and Times of Roller Derby,** Little, Brown, 1971.

DeMott, Benjamin, **You Don't Say: Studies of Modern American Inhibitions,** Harcourt, Brace, Jovanovich, 1966.

Denney, Reuel, **The Astonished Muse: Popular Culture in America,** Universal Library, 1964.

Dichter, Ernest, **Handbook of Consumer Motivations: The Psychology of the World of Objects,** McGraw-Hill, 1964.
**The Strategy of Desire,** Boardman, 1960.

Dorfles, Gillo, **Kitsch: The World of Bad Taste,** Universe Books, 1969.

Dundes, Alan, **Study of Folklore,** Prentice-Hall, 1965.

Egoff, Sheila, G. T. Stubbs, and L. F. Ashley, **Only Connect: Readings on Children's Literature,** Oxford, 1969.

Eisen, Jonathan, ed., **The Age of Rock** (Vols. 1 & 2), Vintage, 1969 & 1970.

Feiffer, Jules, ed., **The Great Comic Book Heroes,** Dial, 1965.

Fishwick, Marshall, and Ray B. Browne, eds., **Icons of Popular Culture,** Bowling Green University Press, 1970.

Frank, Ronald E., et.al., **Purchasing Behavior and Personal Attributes,** University of Pennsylvania Press, 1968.

Freud, Sigmund, **Jokes and Their Relation to the Unconscious,** Norton, 1963.

Gabree, John, **The World of Rock,** Fawcett Gold Medal, 1968.

Galanoy, Terry, **Down the Tube,** Regnery, 1970.

Galewitz, Herb, ed., **The Celebrated Cases of Dick Tracy, 1931-1951** (Chester Gould), Chelsea House, 1970.

Gattegno, Caleb, **Towards a Visual Culture,** Outerbridge and Dienstfrey, 1969.

Geduld, Harry, ed., **Film Maker on Film Making,** Indiana University Press, 1967.

Gelmis, Joseph, **The Film Director as Superstar,** Doubleday, 1970.

Giedion, Siegfried, **Mechanization Takes Command: A Contribution to Anonymous History,** Norton, 1969.

Gleason, Ralph J., **The Jefferson Airplane and the San Francisco Sound,** Ballantine, 1969.

Goldstein, Richard, **The Poetry of Rock,** Bantam, 1969.

Goodstone, Tony, ed., **The Pulps,** Chelsea House, 1970.

Goulart, Ron, **Assault on Childhood,** Shelbourne Press, 1969.

Gray, Harold, **Arf! The Life and Hard Times of Little Orphan Annie, 1933-1945,** Arlington House, 1970.

Grossack, Martin, **Consumer Psychology,** Branden, 1971.

Grotjahn, Martin, **Beyond Laughter: Humor and the Subconscious,** McGraw-Hill, 1966.

Gurko, Leo, **Heroes, Highbrows and the Popular Mind,** Bobbs Merrill, 1953.

Hackett, Alice Payne, **70 Years of Best Sellers,** R. R. Bowker, 1967.

Hagen, Ordean A., ed., **Who Done It: An Encyclopedic Guide to Detective, Mystery and Suspense Fiction,** Bowker, 1969.

Hall, James B., and Barry Ulanov, eds., **Modern Culture and the Arts,** McGraw-Hill, 1967.

Hall, Stuart, and Paddy Whannel, **The Popular Arts: A Critical Guide to the Mass Media,** Beacon Press, 1967.

Harmon, Jim, **Great Radio Comedians,** Doubleday, 1970.

Harper, Ralph, **World of the Thriller,** Case-Western University Press, 1969.

Haycraft, Howard, **Murder for Pleasure: The Life and Times of the Detective Story,** Biblo & Tannen, 1968.

Hoggart, Richard, **The Uses of Literacy: Aspects of Working-Class Life with Special Reference to Publications and Entertainment,** Oxford University Press, 1970.

Holloway, Robert J., et. al. (eds.), **Consumer Behavior: Contemporary Research in Action,** Houghton-Mifflin, 1970.

Hopkins, Jerry, **The Rock Story,** Signet, 1970.

Jacobs, Norman, ed., **Culture for the Millions: Mass Media in Modern Society,** Beacon Press, 1964.

Johnson, Nicholas, **How to Talk Back to Your Television Set,** Little, Brown, 1970.

Jung, Carl J., **Man and His Symbols,** Dell, 1968.

Kael, Pauline, **I Lost It at the Movies,** Bantam, 1966.
   **Kiss Kiss Bang Bang,** Bantam, 1969.

Kerr, Walter, **Tragedy and Comedy,** Simon & Schuster, 1967.

Kiel, Charles, **Urban Blues,** University of Chicago Press, 1966.

Klapp, Orrin E., **Collective Search for Identity,** Holt, Rinehart & Winston, 1969.
   **Heroes, Villains, and Fools: The Changing American Character,** Spectrum, 1962.
   **Symbolic Leaders: Public Dramas and Public Men,** Aldine, 1964.

Knight, Arthur, **The Liveliest Art: A Panoramic History of the Movies,** Macmillan, 1957.

Kouwenhoven, John A., **The Arts in Modern American Civilization,** Norton, 1967 (originally *Made in America,* 1948).

Larrabee, Eric, and Rolf Meyersohn, **Mass Leisure,** Free Press, 1958.

Larsen, Otto N., ed., **Violence and the Mass Media,** Harper & Row, 1968.

Legman, Gershon, **Love and Death: A Study in Censorship,** Hacker, 1963.

Lindgren, Ernest, **The Art of the Film,** Macmillan, 1963.

Lowenthal, Leo, **Literature, Popular Culture and Society,** Pacific Books, 1968.

Lupoff, Dick, and Don Thompson, **All in Color for a Dime,** Arlington House, 1971.

Lynch, William, S.J., **The Image Industries: A Constructive Analysis of Films and Television,** Sheed & Ward, 1959.

McCaffrey, Maurice, **Advertising Wins Elections,** Gilbert Publishing Co., 1962.

McGinniss, Joe, **The Selling of the President, 1968,** Trident, 1969.

McLean, Albert F., Jr., **American Vaudeville As Ritual,** University of Kentucky Press, 1965.

McLuhan, Marshall, **Culture Is Our Business,** McGraw-Hill, 1970.

    **The Mechanical Bride,** Vanguard, 1951.

    **Understanding Media: The Extension of Man,** McGraw-Hill Paperback, 1965.

    **The Gutenberg Galaxy,** University of Toronto Press, 1962.

McLuhan, Marshall, and Quentin Fiore, **War and Peace in the Global Village,** Bantam, 1968.

    **The Medium Is the Massage,** Bantam, 1967.

McLuhan, Marshall, and Harley Parker, **Through the Vanishing Point: Space in Poetry and Painting,** Harper Colophon, 1968.

McQuail, D., **Towards a Sociology of Mass Communications,** Macmillan, 1969.

Malone, Michael E., and Myron Roberts, **From Pop to Culture,** Holt, Rinehart & Winston, 1971.

Mannes, Marya, **But Will It Sell?** Lippincott, 1964.

Marks, J., **Rock and Other Four-Letter Words,** Bantam.

Mayer, Martin, **Madison Avenue, U.S.A.,** Pocket Books, 1959.

Meigs, Cornelia, A. T. Eaton, E. Nesbitt, and R. H. Viguers, **A Critical History of Children's Literature,** Macmillan, 1969.

Melly, George, **Revolt into Styles: The Pop Art,** Doubleday Anchor, 1971.

Mendelsohn, Harold, **Mass Entertainment,** College and University Press, 1966.

Michelson, Herb, **A Very Simple Game: The Story of Roller Derby,** Occasional Publishing Company, 1971.

Morin, Edgar, **The Stars,** Evergreen, 1960.

Murch, Alma E., **Development of the Detective Novel,** Greenwood, 1969.

Nye, Russel: **The Unembarrassed Muse: The Popular Arts in America,** Dial, 1970.

Packard, Vance, **The Hidden Persuaders,** D. McKay, 1957.

Perry, George, and Alan Aldridge, **The Penguin Book of Comics,** Penguin, 1967.

Powdermaker, Hortense, **Hollywood: The Dream Factory,** Little, Brown, 1950.

Reed, Rex, **Do You Sleep in the Nude,** Signet, 1969.

Reik, Theodore, **Jewish Wit,** Gamut Press, 1962.

Rissover, Frederick, and David C. Birch, **Mass Media and the Popular Arts,** McGraw-Hill, 1971.

Rivers, William, **The Opinion Makers,** Beacon Press, 1965.

Rosenberg, Bernard, and David Manning White, **Mass Culture: The Popular Arts in America,** Free Press, 1957.

**Mass Culture Revisited,** Van Nostrand Reinhold, 1971.

Rosenthal, Raymond, ed., **McLuhan: Pro & Con,** Pelican, 1969.

Rosten, Leo C., **Hollywood, The Movie Colony, The Movie Makers,** Harcourt Brace, 1941.

Rowsome, Frank, Jr., **The Verse By the Side of the Road,** Stephen Greene Press, 1965.

Samstag, Nicholas, **How Business Is Bamboozled by the Ad-Boys,** Heineman, 1966.

Sarson, Evelyn, ed., **Action for Children's Television: The First National Symposium on the Effect of Television Programming and Advertising on Children,** Avon, 1971.

Schickel, Richard, **The Disney Version,** Simon & Schuster, 1967.

Schramm, Wilbur, **Television in the Lives of Our Children,** Stanford University Press, 1961.

Seldes, Gilbert, **The Public Arts,** Simon & Schuster, 1956.

Short, Robert L., **The Gospel According to Peanuts,** John Knox Press, 1965.

Siepmann, Charles A., **Radio, Television and Society,** Oxford University Press, 1950.

Smith, George H., **Motivation Research and Marketing,** Greenwood, 1954.

Snelling, O.F., **007 James Bond: A Report,** Signet, 1965.

Sopkin, Charles, **Seven Glorious Days, Seven Fun-Filled Nights,** Simon & Schuster, 1968.

Stearn, Gerald Emanuel ed., **McLuhan: Hot and Cool,** Signet, 1969.

**Superman: From the 30's to the 70's,** Crown Publishers, 1971.

Symons, Julian, **Detective Story in Britain,** British Book Center, 1962.

Thompson, Denys, ed., **Discrimination and Popular Culture,** Penguin, 1964.

Tyler, Parker, **Magic and Myth of the Movies,** Holt, 1947.

Warshow, Robert, **The Immediate Experience,** Anchor, 1964.

Watkins, Julian L., **One Hundred Greatest Ads, Who Wrote Them, and What They Did,** Dover Publications, 1959.

Weinberg, Meyer, **TV in America,** Ballantine, 1962.

Wertham, Frederic, **Seduction of the Innocent,** Rinehart, 1954.

White, David Manning, ed., **Pop Culture in America,** Quadrangle, 1970.

White, David Manning, and Richard Averson, **Sight, Sound and Society: Motion Pictures and Television in America,** Beacon Press, 1968.

White, David Manning, and Robert Abel, eds., **The Funnies: An American Idiom,** Free Press, 1963.

Williams, Paul, ed., **Outlaw Blues,** Dutton, 1969.

Winick, Charles, **The New People,** Pegasus, 1969.

Wolfe, Tom, **The Kandy-Kolored Tangerine-Flake Streamline Baby,** Pocket Books, 1966.

*The Pump House Gang,* Bantam, 1969.

*The Electric Kool-Aid Acid Test,* Bantam, 1969.

Wolfenstein, Martha, and Nathan Leites, **Movies: A Psychological Study,** Free Press, 1950.

---

## Permissions and Sources

The following persons and organizations were very kind to give permission for the use in this volume of essays previously published, for quotations, and for art:

Authority in the Comics: © December, 1966, *Society* magazine, by Transaction, Inc., New Brunswick, New Jersey.

The Man Behind Peanuts and The Secret Significance of Soft Drinks: *Journal of Popular Culture,* Bowling Green State University, Bowling Green, Ohio.

Toying With Children: *Sociology,* University of Pacific, Stockton, California.

Hot Language and Cool Lives: reprinted from *ETC.,* vol. 28, no. 3, by permission of the International Society for General Semantics.

Ads and Addiction: Television Commercials, Drugs and Society: From testimony before a Congressional hearing.

Marvel Comics: Language, Youth, and the Problem of Identity: From *ETC.* with permission. Quotations from Spider-Man used with permission of Stan Lee.

From Peter L. Berger, *Invitation to Sociology,* New York: Doubleday and Co., Inc., quotation in Some Enchanted Evening.

From John G. Cawelti,"The Spillane Phenomenon," University of Chicago Magazine, vol. LXI, no. 5, March/April, 1969, quotation in Who Are Your Heroes?

From Leo Lowenthal, *Literature, Popular Culture, and Society,* Palo Alto, Calif.: Pacific Books. 1968 (first edition 1961), pp. 130-31 (with permission of the publisher), quotation in Hot Language.

From *Newsweek* Magazine, Aug. 18, 1969, part of an article entitled "Advertising's Creative Explosion," quoted in TV Ads and American Society.

From Stuart Hall and Paddy Whannel in *The Popular Arts,* New York: Pantheon Books, Inc., quotation in TV Ads and American Society.

Marvel Comics, and Stan Lee, for permission to use quotations from Spider-Man comics and excerpts of illustrations from Marvel publications. All Spider-Man illustrations © Non-Pareil Publishing Corp., Marvel Comics Group, 625 Madison Avenue, New York, N.Y. 10022.